UNITED STATES FOREIGN POLICY TOWARDS SOUTHERN AFRICA

Andrew Young and Beyond

H. E. Newsum

LeMoyne-Owen College, USA
formerly University of Ife, Nigeria

and

Olayiwola Abegunrin

University of Ife, Nigeria

MACMILLAN

First published 1987

Published by
THE MACMILLAN PRESS LTD
Houndmills, Basingstoke, Hampshire RG21 2XS
and London
Companies and representatives
throughout the world

Printed in Hong Kong

British Library Cataloguing in Publication Data
Newsum, H. E.
United States foreign policy towards Southern
Africa: Andrew Young and beyond.
1. United States – Foreign relations – Africa,
Southern   2. Africa, Southern – Foreign
relations – United States   3. United States
– Foreign relations – 1981–   4. Africa,
Southern – Foreign relations – 1975–
I. Title   II. Abegunrin, Olayiwola
327.73068   E183. 8. A4/
ISBN 0–333–37495–9

This book is dedicated to the freedom fighters of Southern Africa and African American political activists, many of whom have been imprisoned, exiled or have given their lives in the course of their struggles for political independence. Nothing should divide patriots when the nation is in danger. Real independence is hardly given to a people as a gift from their colonial rulers. It has to be fought for in a variety of ways.

Contents

Acknowledgements

We should like to express our gratitude to our families, Lola, Layi Jr and Yetunde Abegunrin, and Obi, Okpara and Chinyere Okafor-Newsum; to our friends, Elise Flowers (typist), Gerald Bennett, Harold Cruse, Aneb Kgositsile (Gloria House), Uri House, Joel Samoff, John Bowen and the Socialist Forum Collective (Ife, Nigeria); and to our colleagues in the Department of International Relations and the Department of English Language at the University of Ife, Nigeria, all of whom offered their unwavering moral support, with some contributing their ideas and skills.

H. E. N.
O. A.

1 The Andrew Young Affair Revisited

When Jimmy Carter appointed Andrew Young to be the US ambassador to the United Nations, black America felt cheated. Africans, similarly, were sceptical. What was Carter trying to achieve? Was the Afro-American vote which sent him to the White House to be placated by a meaningful sinecure or had Carter sensed a strong feeling of Afro-Americans toward Africa that needed a credible mediator in the person of Young? Were US–African relations going to be such a critical factor during Carter's tenure of office that it made diplomatic sense to appoint an Afro-American as ambassador to the United Nations?

This study of Andrew Young and US foreign policy towards Southern Africa has looked into these questions and has come across certain startling observations. It has been argued that Young was appointed ambassador purely to appease him with a sinecure, given his, and black America's, contribution to the Carter victory. Such arguments go further to state that a white president, whether Democrat or Republican, cannot appoint a strong black personality to a prominent cabinet post – for instance, Secretary of HEW, or Defence or State. But this is not the whole story behind Young's appointment: we want to delve deep into the affair and find out what role black personalities have played in the US system of government and how Young fits into it.

There is no doubt that one could say a lot about Andrew Young. However, history has not, at this time, discussed Young in voluminous publications worthy of the best-sellers list. Nor has academia produced a critical textbook in which Young is a focal subject. Thus, the literature of Civil Rights has not devoted any extraordinary attention to Young. Most of the literature written about Andrew Young has been published in popular magazines, paperbacks, journals and newspapers. Therefore, the only available source from which this work has drawn is the popular literature of our time.

1

The work has taken from a small number of biographies, and from popular literature, bits and pieces of eventful information outlining episodes of the Andrew Young affair. A primary aim of this section is to reassess Andrew Young's role in American and world politics.

In spite of several attempts to interview Young, neither he nor his press secretary, Tom Ossenberger, cared to reply our letters. We called his mayoral office at least twice a week for a month and continued to call him periodically. Our calls were always intercepted by Mr Ossenberger, who would inform us that Mr Young had not had time to comment on our request to interview him (see Appendix 1).

Young is important because he is a prototype of US diplomatic personalities and because he represents the final compromise between the black petty-bourgeoisie and the white ruling class. On one side of the compromise, the black petty-bourgeoisie wants to gain an additional share of the American pie. On the other side, a pseudo-liberal section of the white ruling-class elite uses charismatic black personalities such as Andrew Young to take advantage of world sympathy for black Americans and to promote the black American success image in order to entice Africa and the Third World into a web of highly controlled imperialism.

We should note that Malcolm X and the serious nationalists who followed him espoused the belief in the necessity of appealing to the international community for their assistance in making fundamental changes in the American social, political and economic structure by bringing pressure to bear on the United States from the outside. This ideologue rejected the clientage strategy of petty-bourgeois Pan-Africanism with its neocolonial design. We support this view based upon the realisation that the forces of American racism have a stranglehold on mass working-class struggle. It has not been possible for the black American movement to get the support of the white working class, which causes the minority-group movement to be more vulnerable with regard to numerical leverage and to the threat of political liquidation.

Given the polarising-effect which the race factor has on a mass working-class movement in America, international appeal has been perceived as a vital political strategy. The black American movement has appealed particularly to the so-called underdeveloped world, which incidentally has abundant natural resources, and shares with black Americans a common history of oppression based upon economic exploitation by European capitalists. The creation of a platform or organisational base from which this appeal and the activism associated with it could be launched has proved a difficult task. Malcolm X recommended that the black American masses should force this strategy on the United Nations, or the 'World Court' as he referred to it.

Since the Sixth Pan-African Congress in 1974 in Dar es Salaam, the black American position in African world politics has been unclear (if ever it was clear at all). Before this time Dr W. E. B. DuBois had forged an image as the most prolific black American activist in the contemporary Pan-Africanist movement. His devotion to working with Africans on the continent and in the diaspora towards a global political unity of African peoples is on the whole the most impressive attempt of a black American to struggle on behalf of Africa. DuBois was concerned with the forces of colonialism, neocolonialism and imperialism in Africa and how to end them. At the Sixth Pan-African Congress (eleven years after DuBois's death), the rift between the respective proponents of race and class struggle blurred the vision of radical and reformist Africanists on all sides.

The race–class conflict is an outgrowth of numerous attempts to measure the significance of socio-economic class formations (or material factors) over race relations or *vice versa*.

The race question makes special reference to the ability of the white classes mutually to accommodate themselves to a notion of racial superiority. This is particularly true with respect to the historical consistency and cohesiveness of American racism. The race question is also concerned with the dialectic of race supremacy and its corollary psychological manifestations in the racially oppressed. This dialectic is at the core of race inferiority, prejudice and pride (*vis-à-vis* black Americans) and this is a crucial factor in the black American experience which Africans must understand. 'Race pride', under the specific conditions of racism, is a healthy state of mind.

Nevertheless, in our view, race as a basis for explaining social, political and economic evolution has not been a very impressive theorem, unlike explanations linking the evolution of these organisms to the exploitation of land, labour, mineral resources and consumer markets, all of which are primary in the economic lifestyle of a people in both monoracial and multiracial situations. Our persuasion toward class analysis does not, however, preclude race.

Class is the stratification of individuals and groups in society according to the way in which they make their living and according to their social consciousness and lifestyle. Class for the black American is the consequence of slavery and the division of labour between master and slave, on the one hand, and between household workers and field workers, on the other. This is the early formation. In this same respect, class is also a matter of education and the granting of special privileges to the freed slaves of the New England states in the eighteenth century. These slaves, who were the first to learn reading and writing and own property, are the prototypes of the contemporary black American petty-bourgeoisie and the pioneers of entrepreneurial Pan-Africanism. Within the conditions of American capitalism–racism (that is, giving special attention to white race supremacy) all black classes are subordinate to all white classes, although there is collaboration between the black and white upper classes. The concept of class, as regards this work, is a product of the historical and material experience of black Americans as a racially and economically oppressed group, and as a colonially (or neocolonially) controlled national entity in the United States which also has a peculiar internal class structure.

Some Africanists in all camps have expressed concern about the rift between victims of domestic economic and racial oppression and victims of imperialism and neocolonialism – both of which are linked to the material growth of a European super class. The ideological problems which surfaced in the Sixth Pan-African Congress have not been resolved. The tension generated from this conflict is a counter-productive force which is even more dangerous than a plot by the Central Intelligence Agency (CIA) to sabotage genuine attempts to form a radical Pan-African movement.

It was against this background, plus the fact that the black American 'nation', because of its ideological flux, had not produced a statement on the African world predicament agreeable to all its factions and acceptable for consideration by the Organisation for African Unity (OAU) – indeed, no one was pushing this idea anyway – that Andrew Young became the most accessible link between black America and Africa. Young's role (even as a White House appointed figurehead) in US–African affairs was a potential determinant in the further complication of, or resolution to, a seemingly reactionary and counter-productive dialogue between black American and African ideologists. Thus, the role which Young played as a US official, and his role as a private agent trying to make an impact on African affairs, could either have had a positive effect on the Pan-Africanist movement or have been damaging to the image of black American leadership.

But Young's loyalty to the 'democratic' ideals of American capitalism and his flirtation with the neocolonial ruling class of Africa have only shown us that Young does not understand the relationship between Western imperialism and the African national bourgeoisie and the historical role it plays in the question of African liberation along social, economic and political lines.

In the minds of DuBois and Malcolm X, the weakening of imperialism in Africa and the Third World is a step towards the weakening of capitalism and racism in American society. This strategy, however, calls for the purge of petty-bourgeois opportunism and a great sacrifice on the part of the black African masses, who suffer not only from material underdevelopment but also from *ideological underdevelopment*, which is systematically perpetuated under bourgeois democracy.

In our view, the black American concerned with African affairs ought to have an acute awareness of Africa's greatest internal problem, which we believe to be the inevitable struggle between the exploiting black and white minority and the restricted black majority. Any black American with such an awareness, however, could not, or, one hopes, would not, accept a US United Nations post if he intended to develop his awareness and his constituents' awareness to a logical and tangible goal.

The spirit in which we pose the discussion of this work is rooted in the ideals and activism of DuBois and Malcolm X. The kernel of our concern is Pan-African solidarity and the struggle against the exploitative systems of capitalism and imperialism.

I   THE BLACK AMERICAN AND ARMED STRUGGLE IN SOUTHERN AFRICA

The liberation movements of Southern Africa (Mozambique, Angola, Zimbabwe and Namibia) chose armed warfare as the climax of their struggles. While their black American counterparts (specifically those of the professional and entrepreneurial middle class) have found it linguistically and commercially convenient to align themselves with other African nations, such as Liberia, Sierra Leone, Ghana, Kenya and Nigeria, black American politicians, leaders, entrepreneurs and intellectuals have not come to grips with armed struggle in Southern Africa.

Certainly the influence of Western liberal tradition partly explains why armed struggle in Africa has caught black American political, commercial and social elites off guard. It is rare for any member of the black American elite (and this includes the intelligentsia) to support the position of armed confrontation anywhere in Africa or the Third World. This is indicative of the fundamental differences between the protest movement of black America, of which the primary goal has been inclusion in the mainstream of the majority white society, and the struggles of Southern African liberation movements, whose primary goal is black majority rule with a Marxist inclination.

Among the four recent liberation campaigns in Southern Africa, Zimbabwe's has gained the most attention in black America, mainly because Zimbabweans and American blacks share a common language and because Andrew Young was a principal actor in the international negotiations aimed at resolving the eight-year war in that country. Language and politics have likewise married black America and the other African nations which gained independence from Britain, mainly through the parliamentary process. DuBois represented the American 'bride' in that historic wedding.

Given that English is an official language of the Republic of South Africa, and considering the similar histories of racial unrest in that country and the United States, black Americans are undoubtedly interested in the plight of black South Africans as well.

Notwithstanding, the most obvious explanation for the black American's interest in Africa lies in his pursuit of a land base (homeland) and political and commercial leverage in the United States. These seem to be the main tenets of any thoughtful explanation. Evidence for this can be drawn from such examples as Paul Cuffe's Original African Return, the American Colonisation Society, Martin Delaney's Niger Valley expedition, the Garvey movement and Trans-Africa. All these examples, except the last, are also comparable to the migrations of Canadian blacks from Nova Scotia to Sierra Leone.

While forthright political and cultural concerns for Africa may be wanting in some personalities and events associated with Pan-African history, mutual commercial interests have been pursued vigorously (although with minimal success) by black American and African elites.

In a nutshell, it is the peculiar historical relationship between black American and African elites, and the traditional strategies of black American politics, that run counter to the doctrine of armed struggle. The present concern for Africa still seems to be economic (commercial) more than anything else. Black-American elites (politicians, leaders, entrepreneurs and intellectuals) now pursue their interest in Africa under the banners of non-violence, economic pragmatism and balanced interdependence. Hence, under these banners, they perceive themselves as mediators in international relations between the West and Africa. In this connection observers must be increasingly aware of the possibility (or probability) that collaboration between

Western capitalist nations and African elites may supersede the black American's commercial interest and political participation in that arena of international affairs.

II   ON SOCIAL STRATIFICATION AND TERMINOLOGY

Already this work has presented an old problem of social-stratification vocabulary stemming from the works of Karl Marx, Max Weber and the broad community of Western social scientists. We use interchangeably the terms 'middle class', 'petty-bourgeoisie', 'semi-bourgeoisie', 'lumpen-bourgeoisie' and 'comprador'. What these terms have in common is that they all signify a middle group between those who are the principal owners of capital and industry, at the upper level of the social hierarchy, and those who are the real producers of the wealth (labourers), at the lower level.

Certainly the wages and fringe benefits of American assembly-line workers (as well as those of firemen, postmen and others) who have two cars, own split level houses, campers and boats, and pay for their children's college education, have made them a prototype bourgeoisified working class. On the basis of their earnings and some acquired values of the professional sector (the real petty-bourgeoisie), American social science considers them to be a section of the middle class (middle-class workers). Indeed, the pampered American working class causes even more confusion in the determination of social strata and status in contemporary society. Hence a worker who moves from the assembly line to a foreman's position ceases to be a worker from a Marxian point of view, and yet from the standpoint of the managerial staff (the professional sector) he can not be of their same status. That foreman represents a cline in the class system.

When dealing with present-day Africa, the terms mentioned above can cause even more confusion, and among them the term 'middle class' has little or no meaning. In the history of the continent, artisans and petty traders have genuinely occupied the position of a middle section between the aristocracy and peasantry. But the epoch of Western industrialisation and nineteenth-century imperialism has drastically altered the old structure. A more appropriate labelling of major classes in contemporary Africa might be compradors (import/export contractors); the petty-bourgeoisie (permanent secretaries, administrators, traders, university professors, and the managerial staff of private industries);

and labourers and peasants (assembly-line workers, construction workers, civil-service workers and farmers). It would be an oversight not to mention agricultural entrepreneurs, such as H. A. Oluwasanmi of Nigeria, who imports heavy farming-equipment and uses modern farming-techniques. These agricultural entrepreneurs are in the same group as the compradors.

But what does this description of Africa's internal class structure say to our position that the term 'middle class' is inappropriate' in the contemporary African context? The comprador and agricultural-entrepreneur class (and those who could be justifiably grouped with them) are merely peripheral capitalists dependent upon and loyal to the political and economic objectives of Western governments, industrialists and financiers. They themselves are a middle section within the worldwide capitalist economy and in this context they wield very little power. The African comprador and agricultural entrepreneur are petty-bourgeois or semi-bourgeois entities and in an orthodox discussion of international political economy (in spite of their capital ownership) would belong in the same group as permanent secretaries, administrators, university professors, traders, and so on. These comprise the national (internal) petty-bourgeoisie of Africa, which includes the comprador and agricultural-entrepreneur sector, and might in addition be referred to as the 'semi-bourgeoisie' or 'lumpen-bourgeoisie', as E. Franklin Frazier might call them. The real bourgeoisie of Africa is external; it consists of transnational monopoly capitalists and the Western governments that serve their interests and provide foreign aid.

Doubtless, among Marxists, Weberian intellectuals and the wider community of social scientists many would probably disagree with our explanation of class formations. Needless to say, class formations are dynamic and constantly changing. Nevertheless, the basic subject of the ensuing discussion of Andrew Young and American foreign policy towards Southern Africa is the collaboration between the primary owners of capital and industry and the 'middle-class' elites in the worldwide capitalist political economy.

III ANDREW YOUNG: AGENT OF THE CIVIL RIGHTS
     MOVEMENT

Andrew Young sprang from the Civil Rights movement of the 1950s and 1960s. The Civil Rights movement was an integrationist movement which grew out of the black Baptist Church of the American South. Most of its leadership, Young included, came from the pulpit.

The Civil Rights movement gained national attention after the Brown Decision[1] in 1954, which called for state-school desegregation, and the Montgomery bus boycott of 1955, which called for the integration of public transportation in Montgomery, Alabama. In a sense, the Civil Rights movement was a struggle of the oppressed minority groups in the United States. As the largest and as one of the most oppressed of all the minorities, the black community became the centre of conflict for the movement. Through the rhetoric of the prominent Civil Rights spokesman Martin Luther King Jr, the Civil Rights movement later addressed itself to some international issues, particularly the Vietnam war, which boosted the movement's worldwide moral support.

More than a hundred years before the Brown Decision, segregated education was questioned in the case of *Sarah C. Roberts* vs *the City of Boston* (1849). Charles Sumner served as the defending attorney for Miss Roberts, who was forced to attend a black school outside her neighbourhood because she was not allowed to go to a nearby white school. Forty-seven years later legal segregation under the 'separate but equal' doctrine was again questioned, but this time, as in the Montgomery bus boycott, it was in the area of transportation. The 1896 *Plessy* vs *Ferguson* case was a test of the constitutionality of the 1890 Louisiana law providing for separate railway carriages for blacks and whites. In both 1849 and 1896 segregation was upheld.

The Civil Rights movement of the 1950s and 1960s addressed itself to issues directly affecting the black lower class, poor whites and other minority groups; however, this movement from which Andrew Young sprang was far more beneficial to the highly skilled and professional blacks and other affluent minority elements in America. We shall not attempt to judge whether or not the accountability of the Civil Rights movement was philosophically self-centred in a narrow middle-class dream, or whether its main architects, such as Andrew Young, lacked a genuine gut feeling for the plight of the black lower class. We cannot say what is deep in the hearts of men. The racial problem which confronts the black American has been shared by all classes even though some have benefited from the problem itself.

A good many decent, courageous and socially dedicated black Americans participated in the Civil Rights movement. By the same token, a good many black folk were disillusioned by it. The Civil

Rights movement is now history – and is to be judged by its results.

Nevertheless, the movement produced the environment which permitted Andrew Young to be considered for the position of UN ambassador. It is Young's history in the Civil Rights movement which made him an influential figure in politics.

As a member of the Southern Christian Leadership Conference (SCLC), Andrew Young was referred to as 'Uncle Tom' for his negotiating ability, by his colleagues in the inner circle of SCLC leadership. Young was one of Martin Luther King's closest friends and, with King, Ralph Abernathy, Jesse Jackson, Hosea Williams, James Bevels and a few others, Young played a very important role in policy-making within the SCLC as well as devising strategies against the political bureaucracy which they sought to change.

Andrew Young's first political confrontation with top government officials took place in several impromptu meetings between the Civil Rights leadership and Washington bureaucrats, often at the request of President Kennedy in the first instance and then President Johnson. In 1962, when the Federal Bureau of Investigation (FBI) informed President John Kennedy that an adviser to the SCLC, Stanley Levison, was a communist infiltrator, it was Young and King who met with Burke Marshall, then Assistant Attorney-General for Civil Rights, to talk about the allegation.[2] Marshall (who five years later would be called upon again to engineer counter-protest as chairman of the National Advisory Commission on the Selective Service), had received orders from Kennedy to discuss the matter with the two Civil Rights leaders. Before a church congregation Young later reported that the idea of communist infiltration in the Civil Rights movement had no substantive support. The way the story goes, it was Young who demanded that Marshall present sound evidence that there was communist infiltration of the movement.[3] Young's encounters with local-government officials are to be seen against the many arrests which followed major Civil Rights demonstrations all over the United States.

At the moment of Dr King's death, Young, Ralph Abernathy, Jesse Jackson and all the members of the inner circle of the SCLC were there to bear witness to the end of a movement. In the final phase of the Civil Rights movement, Young was one of the principal participants in transforming an unpublicised sanitation strike into a mass demonstration which became national news overnight.[4]

King sent Young and four other top SCLC officials to work with the Memphis Strike Strategy Committee; by this time the Memphis sanitation strike had been running for several weeks.[5] Agitation from the movement's top brass successfully hastened the final outcome of the strike, but lost Dr King in the process. His death proved a shattering blow to mass-movement politics in America.

Since in the Civil Rights movement it was always the intention to put suitably qualified blacks into key positions in the establishment, Young, like a few others, sought to make an impact in government. Andrew Young served in Congress as an elected representative of Georgia until he was appointed UN ambassador in 1976, and in October 1981 he won the mayoral election in Atlanta.

A report published by social activist Dick Gregory and attorney Mark Lane revealed that in 1972, when Young told the public that he wanted a representative post in Congress, the FBI (contemptuous of Civil Rights leaders) considered fabricating grounds for blackmailing Young, thereby destroying his chances of winning a seat in Congress. The FBI eventually decided against this plot and Young won the post.[6] Young was also an active member of the Congressional Black Caucus, which was formed to lobby for concerns of interest to sectors of the black public.

Young's Congressional voting is a far more admirable testimony to his social commitment than is the role he played in carrying out US foreign policy towards Southern Africa. A quantitative analysis of his 1975 Congressional voting-record is provided in Appendix 2. According to statistician Gerald Bennett,[7] 77 per cent of the votes cast by Andrew Young were progressive. His highest progressive rating was on bills covering social areas, i.e. education and welfare (86.86 per cent), and his lowest rating was on bills affecting the government bureaucracy (61.90 per cent). Other areas analysed were the military budget (71.70 per cent), energy bills (64.86 per cent) and bills affecting commerce (73.48 per cent).

Perhaps Young's political race against Stanley Marcus to become mayor of Atlanta reveals the present internal paradox of black electoral politics. The 1981 Atlanta election was a contest between blacks and whites and the substance of the candidates was secondary. Some factions of the black community were not that impressed with Young. But in a showdown between a black and a white most black folk go with the black.[8] Likewise the race between Andrew Young and the white state-representative Stanley Marcus also presented the enduring fact that the white community always goes with the white.

The pool of conflict surrounding the Young–Marcus contest was much deeper than the racial problem, for the conflict also encompassed an intra-class struggle between Atlanta's black and white petty-bourgeois groups (politicians, professionals and entrepreneurs). While the black middle class sought to retain the political apparatuses of municipal power, the white civil superstructure sought to regain city hall so as to consolidate tightly the political machinery and the business sector. According to journalist Tony Brown, one of the most needling issues raised by Young's opponent was an accusation which has been much in evidence in the recent history of black American electoral politics: 'Marcus accused a clique of well-off blacks of benefitting from a black mayor.'[9] And the opposition did not spare former mayor Maynard Jackson in its attacks on the black political leadership. No one denied that the elite section of the Atlanta black middle class had benefited from a black mayor; the same is true of the white middle-class elite when one of their own is occupying the mayoral seat. Tony Brown suggested, however, that, 'If the black middle class continues to prosper and the under class continues to grow, the potential conflict between these two groups could make poor race relations look like the good old days.'[10]

The question of black power for the black community as a whole and the interests of the black petty-bourgeoisie seem to be very much a part of political conflicts in the future. The calling of the black community and the temptations of petty-bourgeois values comprise the paradox of black political struggle. The ability of monopoly capitalists to co-opt the black middle class has been tremendous.

IV DIMINISHING RETURN AND THE SOURCE OF A MALIGN NEGLECT: THE PERIOD AFTER THE CIVIL RIGHTS MOVEMENT

In the early seventies it was already apparent that the legislative remedies aimed at racial polarisation were simply not delivering results. In 1973, the year of the great oil shortage, black Americans suffered from a wave of massive unemployment and have not recovered since. Proportionately blacks have the highest rate of unemployment in America and the rate is steadily rising. In autumn 1981 black unemployment rose to an all-time high of 16.3 per cent and by March 1982 it had risen to a staggering 18 per cent. These figures represent blacks with a history of employment and not those who have never been in the work force; they do not include the black lumpen class. The question before us now is: why aren't the established legislative remedies working? In a nutshell, the problem or paradox involved in compliance with constitutional Civil Rights action is that the Civil Rights movement called for a social system in which race could not be used as a determining factor. Civil Rights leaders used the US Constitution as an example of a faceless document supporting that notion. Now, that same faceless constitution cannot provide the rationale for special arrangements to advance the black cause, notwithstanding Affirmative Action, on a racial basis, even when it seems that it is past racial injustices and the prevailing racism and inequities in American society that have prevented (as Civil Rights supporters see it) the integration of the black public into the American melting-pot.

Before delving any further into a discussion of Andrew Young, let us consider in some general terms the achievements and drawbacks of the Civil Rights movement. Let us also consider the beneficiaries of the movement and those whom one might call the losers.

As mentioned before, the ultimate goal of the movement was to integrate the black race into the American social structure at all levels, giving equal opportunity to all citizens, black and white, on the basis of merit and not race. A special quota system was formed to make up (in a quantitative sense) for past inequities in employment and education. The passing of the Civil Rights Bill and the Voters' Rights Act served as an attempt further to rectify constitutional contradictions. This in turn gave a false sense of security to the black public in an unchanging two-party system under a pseudo-democratic government. Some historians have recorded these out-growths of the Civil Rights movement as achievements, but, if these are achievements, they are only so in a symbolic sense. By this, we mean that the legislation which was passed as a result of the Civil Rights struggle should theoretically have made qualitative and quantitative changes in the black condition. However, we have learned that legislative or state action may have little real effect and is not as important as the civil superstructure, in which the forces of production and upper-class interest are the determining factors of their politico-economic machine. Although blacks succeeded in forcing the state to respond to their call, the American civil structure continues to reject the integrationist programme (although no longer blatantly racist in appearance). In our view, the civil superstructure – the auxiliary of the owners and controllers of the economic base – perceives integration to pose a threat to the dual-labour practices of domestic industries and to the white working and managerial classes, who have historically depended upon and supported the white capital-owning class.

The overwhelming resistance to the black movement from the racist and conservative white professional middle class and from the larger white non-professional middle class has made compliance with the Civil Rights mandate virtually impossible. After the Civil Rights heyday, these elements of the American public twice voted Richard Nixon to the presidency and are now believed to be Ronald Reagan's most devoted supporters.

The integration of state schools was undermined by white flight to the outer areas of the cities. Most higher-education institutions have never satisfied their quota requirements, but instead offer elaborate proposals on how to achieve the desired result. The quota system has been viciously attacked in university education. The Bakke Case, in which a thirty-seven year old white male complained that he had been unjustly refused admission to a California university, argued that, while minorities were entering predominantly white schools through the quota system, qualified whites were being turned away. Bakke claimed 'REVERSE DISCRIMINATION' and won his case in accordance with the Constitution. Black enrolment in higher education reached its all-time peak during the sixties but has been dropping since.

DuBois predicted (and correctly so) that the 1954 Brown decision, which called for state-school desegregation, would lead to the unemployment of many of the nation's black teachers, as they were inevitably replaced by whites, and would interrupt the cultural stability which had prevailed in black educational institutions, so making whites the primary beneficiaries of a long list of Civil Rights actions.[11]

Thus, after many blacks, seeking 'new opportunities', migrated northward in the thirties and fifties, plantation-owners in the Southern states benefited because black labour was replaced by cheaper mechanical labour and illegal migrant workers.

The legislative 'achievements' of the Civil Rights movement and the shattering of the Jim Crow system created a cover which masked the deeply ingrained contradictions in America. During a period when the world was experiencing a cold war between the two major super powers, revolutions in China and in Cuba and nationalism in Africa, the superficial achievements of Civil Rights made the United States look progressive to the new national entities which were coming into being in the underdeveloped world, and in our opinion the spotlighting of Andrew Young took place in order to create a similar illusion.

The black youth of the late seventies, and now of the eighties, have been steered away from the black struggle. Their most potent concerns are for tinsel prestige, individual status, and fun and games.

The Civil Rights movement was followed by a period of 'benign neglect'. This strategy was the brainchild of Daniel Moynihan, a former Harvard professor turned senator for New York State. In a report to President Johnson and later President Nixon, Moynihan suggested that the nation would benefit from a period of benign neglect in which the media would remove the black-militant presence from public view, while at the same time pumping money into the black middle class. The implementation of Moynihan's proposal, particularly the funding of black businesses, created an illusion of racial peace between 1968 and 1972. The façade showed the establishment's belief that token acts of appeasement provide evidence of effective racial remedies, but this is mere compensation for the lax enforcement of Civil Rights.

After a while it was clear to some people that it was the built-in opportunism of the Civil Rights movement which partly accounted for its bankruptcy. After all, why shouldn't a ruling class which claims to be democratic accept into its fold members of the influential black petty-bourgeoisie – the marginal men such as Andrew Young – when it had always done so?

V ANDREW YOUNG THE HERO

The overwhelming enthusiasm with which publishers welcomed the hero-worship of Andrew Young is evident in the four or five biographies written about him and published between 1978 and 1980. The titles of some of these books demonstrate the notoriety attached to the hero. *Andrew Young: Biography of a Realist*, *Andrew Young: Man with a Mission* and *Andrew Young: The Impossible Man* are examples of these works and each rings with excitement. All of the biographies, aimed at an audience ranging from primary-school children to adults, tell the story of the boy most likely to succeed: Andrew Young, who sprang from the comfortable household of a middle-class black family in an all-white neighbourhood, to the citadel chambers of American politics. In addition to hero-worshipping, these biographies are full of praise for the Carter Administration.

It is quite understandable that a black middle-class figure head such as Young should become a subject of hero-worship. The progress of the black petty-bourgeoisie, as well as the progress of the American petty-bourgeoisie as a whole, has always been a measure of success. Middle-class success stories have served as examples of the virtues of capitalism. But the social code 'work hard and succeed' has traditionally ignored the built-in inequalities perpetuated by the two-headed monster of 'civil and institutionalised' racism and sexism in the American capitalist system. Thus, the onslaught of inflation and high interest rates is turning sectors of the so-called middle class into the working poor. The non-professional middle class is becoming a victim of increased underemployment and unemployment.

Perhaps the tremendous faith which blacks have in the private free-enterprise model, which has rendered them ignorant, unsophisticated disciples of anti-communist and anti-socialist propaganda, is a far greater enemy to them than the powerless black middle class. It is necessary to force apart the structural pillars and dissolve the ideological foundation upon which this faith is founded.

To many black Americans, Young is indeed a hero. As UN ambassador, Young made many assertions about issues which, in the past, had been avoided by US officials. Some of these assertions provoked the white conservative elements of the American public. But while white conservatives became increasingly upset with Young, his popularity among blacks rose. Thus the attention which Young attracted to Africa raised popular awareness about the continent, as well as implications for a new bourgeois Pan-Africanist integrationist movement in black America.

When Young pointed out that America had political prisoners and came under attack by the press and some government officials, black Americans rallied behind him. What Young had done was tactical; it was his way of focusing international attention on the Wilmington Ten Case. This was a legal proceeding involving nine blacks and one white who were alleged to have burned down commercial property during the 1971 Civil Rights demonstration in Wilmington, North Carolina. Young's statement about America having political prisoners opened the door to discussion of the case and other acts of injustice imposed upon black Americans.

Nevertheless, Andrew Young, Jimmy Carter and a few other black and white leaders did not wield enough influence to curtail the racial violence which followed the McDuffie slaying in Miami, Florida, which led to 1200 arrests between 16 and 21 May 1980.

The programme which Young, Randall Robinson, Charles Diggs (whose record, as compared to Young's, reveals a more genuine commitment to exposing international political contradictions) and some other middle-class blacks put together under the banner of the TransAfrica organisation was directed at launching a small but influential social movement whose power base was rooted in the ability of the black American international bourgeoisie (Young and others) to manipulate both African and Third World interests on the one hand, and the US interests on the other. It was not a new idea to use Africa to advance the black American cause.

Progressive Pan-Africanist nationalists have for a long time believed that the hostile racist environment of America would not permit blacks to form a solid power base from that country's resources. They held that the rights of black Americans would be determined by African liberation and the successful struggles of oppressed people throughout the world. What is new about the Pan-Africanism of TransAfrica is the catalyst which is carrying the idea and popularising it within the black American 'nation'.

After the Garvey movement, the ideals of Pan-Africanism were advocated by Dr W. E. B. Dubois, who had been actively involved in the Pan-African movement since the turn of the century. Dubois was mainly concerned with ending colonialism and establishing national independence throughout Africa. Pan-Africanist ideals also came from a few withdrawn or obscure radical intellectuals and filtered down into the grass-roots movement using a kind of rhetoric which attempted to remove class identification. Following the example of the nationalist leader Malcolm X, the progressive nationalists believe in (and try to follow, though not always successfully) a programme which includes all classes, with a steering-committee representing the collective interest of the whole community and not just the interest of a select few. Because these nationalists followed the notion of a working-class or 'grass-roots' movement directed at making fundamental changes in the American political and economic structure and at improving the black condition from the 'bottom up', some political theorists have labelled them 'progressive' to distinguish them from the reactionary petit-bourgeois nationalists.

History tells us that the black American entrepreneur, more than anyone else, knows from past attempts that black businesses simply do not have the means to establish a market between Africa and the black American 'nation'. If this is true then it seems that the entrepreneurial/professional class represented by Young, the 'black component' of the Overseas Private Investment Corporation (OPIC) – under the Carter Administration – and TransAfrica, have evidently misread the text along the way. In the present predicament, the black American petty-bourgeoisie can do nothing more than make Africans economic clients and doubtless victims of the United States. In his book *The Crisis of the Negro Intellectual*, Harold Cruse points out that, while Garvey suggested black capitalism for Africa in the 1920s, the rest of the underdeveloped world was moving from anti-imperialism to anti-capitalism. Cruse's analysis of Garvey's back-to-Africa movement can be applied to bourgeois Pan-Africanists of the present period. In recent decades not only have the millions of Africans in Tanzania, Mozambique, Angola and Zimbabwe demonstrated a willingness to make sacrifices for liberation, but their governments have also rejected capitalism, notwithstanding their pragmatic ties to capitalist countries and the rough task of pursuing a socialist democracy. All evidence points to the fact that Young and others like him are carrying on Garveyism minus the ideas of racial separatism and physical migration to the motherland. This is certainly not the Pan-Africanism articulated by Dubois and Nkrumah, who understood the class struggle on the African continent, or by the progressive nationalist organisations which emerged in the sixties.

The Pan-Africanist views of the progressive nationalist organisations which formed before TransAfrica do not include collaboration with the international capitalist class in their programmes for African liberation. In fact, these Pan-Africanist nationalists are racial separatists who have such a cynical view of the white controlling class that, on the basis of ideological principles, they have limited their contribution to African liberation to what they can achieve with their own organisational resources. From what one can tell of what the progressive nationalists think about Africa in terms of international political economic relations, the resolution pronounced in Tanzania's Arusha Declaration of 1967, and practised in that country since 1964, concerning a foreign policy of positive non-alignment or, in our words, *aid from external sources with no strings attached*, seems to represent their line fairly well.

The degree to which Young, J. Bruce Llewellyn (former president of OPIC) or TransAfrica would, if given the opportunity, seduce African nations into disadvantageous ties with the Western ruling class is in no way comparable to what is intended by the Arusha Declaration. This is clear from what Young, in particular, has said and done so far.

If those black Americans who consider Young a hero would look at history, they would see that Young's new middle-class 'social move-ment', like the Civil Rights movement, will not in the long run benefit the black lower classes, who are in real need of liberation. It appears that what Andrew Young has in mind for the next stage will only benefit the black American and African business elites and the Third World bourgeoisie, on the one hand, and the Western ruling class, on the other.

This middle-class movement in which Andrew Young is so im-pressive does not have the appeal of a mass movement. The way we see it, it is difficult to imagine that the black lower classes actually see themselves as part of Young's new programme. We believe that black Americans feel that Young's success is an outgrowth of their sacrifices in the social demonstrations of the 1960s. It is not at all clear what the larger black American public thinks of Young's relationship with African elites and Western transnational business. Such behaviour has been reduced to the popular idiom 'getting over'. What is clear to some observers is that, though the black masses played a significant role as the rank and file of Civil Rights demonstrations in the 'non-violent but violent' movement of the sixties, they are no longer important to the small social movement now being forged by the black middle class. This new movement is not a humanistic venture. It is located in the self-interest of the black petit-bourgeoisie.

What black Americans need to see now is that Young is an agent of petty-bourgeois opportunism characterised by status-seeking social climbers and deference politics, manipulated by the corporate elites and a 'Dixieland'-style 'democrat' (former President Carter) whose political career is clearly one which has served big business and the anti-Union position in the American South.

Young was to Carter what Booker T. Washington was to Carnegie during the period of Reconstruction in the late nineteenth century. To our knowledge, there is nothing in Carter's background, particu-larly when Governor of Georgia, that would support the notion that he could return black folk to the grand (but illusory) 'golden ages' of the Roosevelt, Kennedy and Johnson eras. In fact, these 'golden ages' were nothing more than brief periods of appeasement: for instance, during the 1960s large sums from Federal funds were used (and eventually exhausted) for social-welfare programmes such as Model Cities, the War on Poverty and other community development organisations which have died or are dying. The period which follows a 'golden age' always introduces economic repercussions which hit the black community the hardest. Perhaps the greatest damage done by these 'golden ages' is that they strangle the potential for self-reliance among suppressed groups. The 1970s and 1980s exemplify such a period. The 1970s, with high inflation and unemployment, can be considered the *dark age* that followed the 1960s.

The longest footnote in this chapter of American history will show how during the Carter Administration the conditions of the black American community became progressively worse in spite of campaign promises.

Because of the support of Young, Mrs Coretta King and Martin Luther King Sr (the wife and father of the late Dr King), the black vote put Carter in the White House. Though Young openly claimed he was not interested in a presidential appointment, Carter let it be known through media sources that Young was a likely candidate for a major post in his administration.

When Young met with some of the nation's top black elected officials and political activists shortly after Carter's election in 1976, he talked about strategic posts in Carter's administration which blacks should pursue. Young made it clear that blacks could gain nothing from the UN-ambassador post. But, the fact is that, shortly after this meeting, Young accepted that very position.[12]

Young used the UN ambassadorship and his influence on the suppressed masses to advance the ideological and economic mission of world capitalism at the inevitable expense of the world's oppressed classes. In the long run, what he did as an international figure can only cause the greatest distrust between black Americans and the international struggle.

Andrew Young has been consistent in his use of client, opposition and deference tactics (these will be discussed later) to gain acceptance into mainstream America. As in the days of the Civil Rights movement, Andrew Young is still trying to fulfil a dream rooted in the expansionist, labour contemptuous ideals and practices of Western capitalism. Andrew Young is a middle-class middleman involved in the oppressor's parasitic relationship with the oppressed. The position which Young holds is historically typical of the petty-bourgeoisie.

VI THE TRILATERAL COMMISSION: IMPLICATIONS FOR FOREIGN-POLICY-MAKING IN THE CARTER ADMINISTRATION

Around 1973 the Trilateral Commission was formed to address certain international issues affecting world capitalism. The Commission's principal organisers were David Rockefeller of the Chase Manhattan Bank; Milton Katz, director of International legal Studies at Harvard; and Zbigniew Brzezinski, former US National Security Adviser to President Carter. It is obvious that one of these gentlemen was directly linked to the Carter Administration. The other two (Rockefeller and Katz) have directly influenced US foreign relations. Jimmy Carter was brought into the group shortly after it was formed and became a member of its governing board.[13] More important to this discussion, Young also became a member of this commission in 1973, and two of the Commission's key members (Carter and Brzezinski) were in positions that directly influenced Andrew Young as a principal representative of US foreign policy.

The ultimate aim or motivating force behind the Trilateral Commission was

(1) to formulate a united front for advancing capitalism;
(2) to minimise socialist influence in the so-called developing world;[14]
(3) to contain and control the liberation movement in Africa and the Middle East; and
(4) to curb the economic problems of unemployment and inflation within the United States.[15]

Among its distinguished participants from America's allies we find the Vice-President of the Bank of Tokyo; the head of the Nissan Motor Company; The Presidents of Hitachi, Mitsubishi and Sony; the President of the Bank of Paris; the head of Fiat; and the President of the West German Chamber of Commerce. This list is by no means complete. Americans in the Trilateral Commission included: representatives of Exxon; the Editor and Chief of Time Incorporated; Steelworkers' President I. W. Abel; the President of Coca-Cola, J. Paul Austin; the chairmen of Sears and Roebuck; the presidents of the Bank of America, Wells Fargo and Chase Manhattan Bank; and former Secretary of State Henry Kissinger.[16]

The mandate of the Trilateral Commission was directly focused on international affairs. It is in this type of citadel of international politico–economic activity that foreign policy is conceived. The aims of the Trilateral Commission were compatible with the objectives of some US foreign-policy documents, which will be discussed later in this work. It is believed that the implied connection between the Trilateral Commission, the Carter Administration and US foreign policy may be useful in shaping our perspective on Andrew Young.

VII   ANDREW YOUNG THE AMBASSADOR: IMPLICATIONS FOR US FOREIGN POLICY

A study of the connection between Young, the Civil Rights movement and the period 1968–76 is, in a fundamental sense, a prerequisite for understanding Young's political mind and activities.

What is Andrew Young about? His basic political thinking can be traced to two political strategies. The first is that of playing the role of *client* to some external source. This strategy can be traced to Booker T. Washington and may be called 'deference politics'. The second strategy, *opposition*, which calls for flirtation with the external bourgeoisie, is like clientage in one way and unlike it in another. Like clientage, it believes that collaboration between the client and the ruling class is inescapable; but, unlike it, it 'defiantly' and 'militantly' attempts to implement rules and norms which its practitioners can, as they see it, validly claim to share with the establishment which they seek to change. In the special case of black–white relations in America, opposition politics is used to mobilise whatever white support can be rallied by blacks on behalf of their constitutional and democratic rights.[17] Members of both the SCLC and NAACP (National Association for the Advancement of Colored People) can be said to be among its most impressive practitioners.

Although Young and others in the Civil Rights movement sought to activate forces changing in some way the conventional political structure, they did not alter, in any fundamental way, the apparatus of American capitalism and imperialism. The Civil Rights movement appealed to the moral fibre of the Christian populace and to liberal reformists. And, though the American conservatives criticised his appointment to the United Nations, it is this same Christian–liberal constituency which supported Young from 1977 to 1979, and from whose point of view we can understand Young's vocal but moderate stance on African and Third World affairs. It is our guess, and probably accurate, that Young's most committed supporters and sponsors are petty-bourgeois blacks and whites and liberal capitalists.

In a transcribed interview published in *Africa* magazine in October 1979, Young was asked, in the light of the decision by the United States to allow the Muzorewa regime to open a legation in Washington, if his resignation as US ambassador to the United Nations threatened the current policy toward Africa. Young first replied with confidence that his successor, Donald McHenry, would not allow any such policy reversal; but what he went on to say is far more interesting than any confidence he might ever have evoked in US African policy.

Young pointed out that his influence in American–African affairs would be even greater as a free agent able to say and do what he liked. He spoke of mobilising the black American public (particularly the middle class) around the issue of US policy in relation to African politics and economic 'development'. The groundwork for mobilising these forces had already begun.

TransAfrica, an organisation which emerged from the 1976 Black-Leadership Conference on Africa, which attracted the interest of black American entrepreneurs, formed a lobby committed to educating the public about African and Caribbean affairs, particularly the issues surrounding Zimbabwe (then Rhodesia), South Africa and Namibia. Subsequently, TransAfrica and other petty-bourgeois organisations, such as the National Business League (NBL), the Overseas Private Investment Corporation (OPIC) under J. Bruce Llewellyn,[18] and Young's own Young Ideas Incorporated became concerned with creating a liaison between black and white American business folk and the African market. Given the peculiar history of black political thought in America, a philosophy of 'interdependent capitalism with a conscience' might be extracted from the collective thinking of this 'coalition'. In his interview with *Africa* and in his speech to the Nigerian–American Chamber of Commerce in September 1979,[19] Young illustrated this philosophical view.

In the interview published by *Africa*, Young attempted to give concrete examples of the liaison between black America and Africa. He said, for instance, that, if the American system of public education, and especially 'the black component' of it, was relevant to what Nigeria was trying to do with its Universal Primary Education (UPE) scheme,[20] then white and black American entrepreneurs and Nigerian leaders should explore the possibility of Nigeria producing textbooks cheaply. Now what does this mean? What should we understand to be the connection between 'the black component of the US public school system' and producing textbooks in Nigeria or any other part of Africa? Given that the cultural realities of Africans and black Americans are quite different, is it worthwhile considering the black component in American education when planning educational development in Nigeria? (The tail wagging the dog, so to speak.)

What was meant by 'the black component' of the American public-education system was not clear. Black American educationalists have made some advances in teaching-methods applied to the underprivileged black child and in introducing black history, sociology, politics and literature into the mainstream curriculum. In addition, black writers of children's literature have projected more positive images of black people in their works and these works are now more readily used in classrooms. Nevertheless, these developments have been geared toward theory and content; black Americans have not played a dominant role in the production and marketing of educational texts.

Nigeria has an educated class capable of theorising on education and of supplying educational materials. Some Nigerian educationalists and leaders believe that, since it could be argued that local Nigerian printers would find it difficult to satisfy the demand for textbooks in Ibadan alone, for the UPE scheme to succeed much must be done to increase textbook production, as well as expand educational facilities generally. They are also convinced that what Nigeria needs is a big injection of technically advanced hardware, industrial know-how and marketing-expertise to establish a printing-industry to serve the various state governments. Although some black Americans may have a degree of industrial know-how and marketing-expertise, they do not control the means that would provide the desired hardware.

More resourcefully, other Nigerians might hold that the rapid increase of small jobbing printers in Nigeria shows great promise for the inexpensive production of sufficient textbooks in the future. An initial period of capital stimulation (state subsidy) and the subsequent collectivisation and socialisation of small printing-shops might remedy the expense of importing teaching-texts to Nigeria, and may be a viable alternative to a centralised printing-industry tied to American technology. However, a resolution proposing this would be perceived as 'Maoist–Leninist' and downright impractical by the Nigerian neo-colonial ruling class.

But how practical was Andrew Young's suggestion that Nigerians and black Americans – and inevitably whites too – should explore the possibility of Nigeria producing textbooks cheaply? Can this brand of economic Pan-Africanism avoid the web of 'unevendependency' which permeates the power relations of international affairs?

Black Americans have not been able to establish a strong network of printers or publishers within the United States. In the 1960s, when black literature was in vogue, black publications were controlled by white publishers such as Putnam, Bantam, Doubleday, Morrow and Vintage. In the past decade, financial constraints have forced some black American newspaper companies to go from daily to weekly publications. Again, most black American publishers, including Johnson Publications, have their materials printed by white printers. The Nation of Islam, under Elijah Muhammad, is the only black American organisation which has provided an example of a relatively independent black press. Since the black-consciousness movement lost its momentum in the 1970s, many black American writers find it difficult to get their manuscripts accepted for publication. Several black publications produced in the sixties are now going out of print with no forseeable possibility of being reprinted.

Young sees black Americans helping African nations select from the American 'supermarket' (a role to be partially fulfilled by his Young Ideas Incorporated) things that are useful to them and avoid those things that are not. On the surface, this is an admirable objective. While Africa is undergoing the long process of developing its industrial and technological base, there is a need for strict policies with regard to technological transfers and merchandise selection. But the role of the black American 'middle man', who seems to be an important element in the triangle, also raises implications from which we can establish a basic truth about the black American petty-bourgeoisie and their political strategies of clientage and opposition. The black–white American–African relationship, as Young sees it, will in the final analysis follow the principles or rule of thumb of the Civil Rights movement. To him, the underdevelopment of blacks in the diaspora and on the continent can be overcome by the same tactics – which, in this case means finding a basis for interracial and international collaboration by choosing political and economic objectives which the more influential outsiders – Western industrialists and financiers – will support.[21]

When addressing the Nigerian–American Chamber of Commerce, Young illuminated his confidence in interracial collaboration and economic Pan-Africanism. Speaking on the Union Carbide project in Kano, Nigeria, he said,

Union Carbide's project . . . has been successful, in part, because there's a team of a black American and a white American working together with Nigerians to develop a very sophisticated and profitable business enterprise. Where we have tried to go in with white Americans alone without black Americans, we've not been as successful. And where we have tried to go in without adequate Nigerian partnership and consultation we have not been as successful.[22]

But, when making this remark, was Young unaware that the twenty-year-old Union Carbide project had not yet had any real impact on the problems of disease, communal and commercial underdevelopment, and political turmoil in the Kano area? Let's hope not. We might rather assume that Young's speech was tailored for the audience he was addressing.

From the very beginning, when Young was appointed ambassador to the United Nations, his clientage–opposition tactics were evident in relation to Southern African affairs. In 1977 Young suggested[23] that the United States should support a programme to train indigenous black leaders to govern South Africa once the country was under majority rule. This is no less than the kind of ideal scheme that Western imperialism needs to establish a neocolonial regime in Southern Africa. Our worst fear is that Young was possibly suggesting another Anglo-American plan (formerly called 'Rhodesia: Proposals for a Settlement') for South Africa. The basis for this fear is linked to the fact that Young and British Foreign Secretary David Owen acted as the main salesmen of the Anglo-American Proposals (see Appendix 3 for the text).

As we know, the Anglo-American Proposals made the United States and the British crown the protectors of Zimbabwean interests while the country underwent a transition to black majority rule. But whose interests were really to be protected? The Proposals guaranteed Ian Smith's party twenty seats in the Parliament. The voting-power of these seats was intended to protect white-minority-owned industries against nationalisation (see also Annex C).[24] This was certainly a departure from the West's attitudes to oppressive regimes and war criminals in Europe after the Second World War. Thus, the Anglo-American plan made open negotiations for a security force comprising all the country's armed and police forces, including the predominantly white racist police force of the former Smith regime and even the South African troops and mercenaries that had supported it.

Thus, a provision whereby Smith's police force might continue exercising its power against Mugabe's and Nkomo's armies and supporters was also subject to debate. This was the most crucial factor in the overall scheme.

When we look carefully at the Anglo-American plan and consider the suffering of black Zimbabweans at the hands of white Rhodesians, one must seriously ponder how Andrew Young, Britain, the United States and Nigeria[25] could propose such a compromise.

Since so many African liberation support groups have been waiting for the majority-rule ideology to take effect in South Africa, Young began to speculate on that country's future. Perhaps these speculations were meant to bring 'soul' or 'magic' into the stalemate diplomacy on South Africa. Even so, we must understand that one of Young's basic functions was to make the US imperialist design appealing to Africans. What Young was talking about with regard to a black-leadership training-programme in South Africa was the icing on the cake. Here Young implied the final compromise between the black upper class and the white ruling class in Africa. Young's suggestion of a US-trained black government in South Africa is parallel to what happened after the Civil Rights era in America, with the emergence of black mayors and congressmen in some American cities. [26]

In trying to understand Young's line of thinking about US-trained black leaders in South Africa, let us turn to the black political scene in America, for this was Young's most obvious frame of reference. First one needs to ask what black Americans hope to gain from their participation in American electoral politics.

Presumably the expected gain is increased political power for black middle-class professionals who claim to be concerned about resolving the problems of poor housing, inefficient funding for education, unemployment and inflation, among other things. However, as black middle-class professionals gain more prestigious positions in the US electoral system, blacks as a whole are no less cut off from the political and economic mainstreams of society. The problems of housing, education, unemployment and inflation persist and even grow worse. It is not necessarily black politicians who are the problem, though: it is the political structure itself, along with monopoly capitalism, that aggravates America's social and economic problems.

Still, what is wrong with black politicians in America? Black middle-class elites pursue political office mainly to satisfy the petty-bourgeois fetish of prestige. Their political failings stem from the fact that, to them, the holding of public office is mainly a matter of social standing.

Speaking on black American politics in the 1980s, political scientist Charles V. Hamilton said that 'positions' (offices), not policies, are the main concern of black politicians.[27] Hamilton forecast that by the end of the decade we will probably see 'two black senators, ten more blacks in the House of Representatives' and 'a combination of shouting and whispering, badgering and bargaining'.[28] He predicted that black participation in electoral politics will swell in Southern states such as Alabama, Louisiana, Mississippi, Georgia, North Carolina, South Carolina and Virginia.[29] Perhaps at the time, Hamilton could not predict that this swelling black population would be triggered by the Jackson Campaign.

Where we find blacks holding major offices (particularly mayoral offices), in local political structures, we discover that whites adopt a policy of tactical withdrawal. The local white business elites concentrate on maintaining a strong and profitable economic base, and determine the power relations in the local area. Neighbourhood leaders in the white community (suburbs) form civic organisations that influence state and Federal politics – with little regard for the 'black inner city' or even in direct opposition to it.

Black public-office holders must be accountable to all groups belonging to their constituency – blacks and whites, rich and poor. Therefore, the extent to which black politicians can actually offer a better deal to the black masses lies in the checks and balances of this social dialectic. The swelling participation of blacks in American electoral politics does not seem to be a solution or an overriding problem. It is, however, deception. The major problem seems to be an eroding capitalist economy. To put it another way, the problem is a ruling class selfishly fixated on anti-labour technology. And with this is an unwillingness, at all levels, to collectivise and socialise the private sector.

Since the black professional middle class has always played a client role in the reproduction of the capitalist political economy, it follows that the ability of that class to offer a better deal to the black masses is also tied to the crisis of American capitalism. The participation of black American elites in American electoral politics, and their relationship to the inner-city black public characterises one example of domestic neocolonialism. The only real power of neocolonial rule is deception, and in some cases violence.

Because Andrew Young is anti-racist, he supports the principle of majority rule and opposes the white minority regime in South Africa. But also, because Young is pro-capitalist, his antidote to the present

African situation is neocolonial. Again, we recognise that his view on US Southern Africa policy is a reflection of the clientage and opposition strategies of the Civil Rights movement. When we look at him as a black American politician and when we look at the position of blacks in the American political system, we see that the neocolonial stage is seen by some black Americans as final, even if unfortunate. In America, the black middle class has become quite comfortable with deference and marginal politics. Throughout the evolution of this neocolonial structure in American society, the black American lower-class groups have become more and more alienated from American political and economic structures. Notwithstanding some small, low-key progressive movements, the neocolonial preoccupations of middle-class blacks within the American political system made deference politics and clientage focal characteristics of black-American political strategy. It is against this background that we must examine Andrew Young's role in Southern Africa.

While the United States was proposing the Anglo-American plan in Zimbabwe, it was also heavily engaged in supplying arms to both the Smith regime and South Africa.[30] The implication was that the two racist regimes would provide each other with the necessary back-up whenever the time came to take drastic measures against the liberation struggle. The combination of a strong fascist military inside South Africa and possibly Namibia, and a privileged settler community and a racist police force in Zimbabwe could have provided a power base in Southern Africa aimed at destroying the liberation movement – and with it, the two major socialist organisations, the Popular Movement for the Liberation of Angola (MPLA) and the Mozambique Liberation Front (Frelimo), who have assumed state power in Angola and Mozambique respectively.

If the US State Department had accepted Andrew Young's suggestion for a US-trained black government in South Africa under a kind of Anglo-American settlement for the white South African settlers, we should have had the complete neocolonial design for Southern Africa. In the total package, with both South Africa and Zimbabwe[31] under a neocolonial rule controlled from outside, both having fascist police and military forces, privileged settler communities and black puppet regimes, the expansion of the liberation movement would have become even more difficult.

Both Young's idea on a black-leadership training-programme in South Africa and the Anglo-American plan had implications which were consistent with the Trilateral Commission mandate, particularly

those aspects which called for the containment and control of liberation struggles in Africa, and the minimisation of socialist influences in
the 'developing' world.

During his career as ambassador, and particularly in the first year,
Young made several extraordinary pronouncements, most of which
implied a US dominance in Africa. Again, in 1977 – he suggested a
US supported 'anti-apartheid newspaper' in South Africa. This
would have given the United States an opportunity to control the
mass media in Southern Africa and thereby control public opinion.[32]

We commended Young in 1977, when he argued that the United
States should have ties with the socialist MPLA government in
Angola. Young's statement seemed to set the White House on the
right course with regard to Angola. Young played down the notion
that Soviet–Cuban influence in Angola posed a threat to Western
interests. He argued that, since Angola had become independent as
recently as 1975, and was like any other developing nation, it would
need strong economic relations with more developed countries before it could efficiently provide for its people as an independent state.
Young argued that US aid to Angola could only improve relations
between the two countries.[33]

Again, while black politicians and action groups and several African officials praised Young, white American politicians and other
conservatives attacked him from all sides. Since the installation of the
MPLA government and the intervention of 18,000 Cuban troops in
Angola in 1975 – during a period, after independence, when fighting
started between the MPLA and rebel forces – some Washington
officials had been very concerned about the spread of socialist influence in Africa. In January 1976, Kissinger had claimed that the
Soviets had given $200 million in aid to Angola.[34] Also, conservative
elements had not recovered from the execution of four white mercenaries and the imprisonment of nine others in Angola in June 1976.

Young's thinking about socialist influence, however, was quite
contrary to the conservative point of view. First of all, it seemed that
he acknowledged that the MPLA was the popular faction and the
legitimate government of Angola. Second, he saw the Soviet–Cuban
influence in Angola as a stabilising force in the country. Owing to
pressures from conservative elements, Young later explained that by
this he meant that the USSR and Cuba had contributed generally to
Angola's development. Whatever he did mean, he keyed in on the
fact that Cuban troops were protecting Gulf's oil installations in
Angola during the country's most troubled period.

The conservative reactions to Young's pronouncements were predictable: they were straight East–West cold-war sentiments egged on by the then National Security Adviser, Zbigniew Brzezinski. But these reactions from the white establishment – combined with the contrariness of Ambassador Young, stirred up a kind of controversy (at least in the mass media), which, for some of us, created illusions of hope concerning US policy on Africa. Our hopes and the overall public concern for US foreign policy were no doubt anticipated by the policy-makers. Either by coincidence or by design, the political flux of the Carter Administration presented the public with all its hopes and every disappointment.

If it appeared that the United States had a change of heart toward Angola (or Africa in general) during Young's ambassadorship, then we should ask ourselves if this change was not just a case of imperialist opportunism. Young effectively carried out the unclear political mission of bringing the US and Africa closer together. But this closeness between the two worlds was based not on altruism, but rather on the principle of 'business as usual'. More positive relationships with black African states are possibly the real key to protecting Western economic interests on the continent. The credit due for the relaxation of the US approach to Angola can not, however, go to Andrew Young: the influence of Gulf Oil on the State Department must not be overlooked.

Gulf Oil clearly supported the MPLA in 1975 during the transitional period from Portuguese rule to majority rule. Gulf realised that the MPLA was the popular faction in Angola, and the likely successor to the Portuguese regime. Gulf's position on the Angola matter was well known to the State Department and the two parties exchanged advice on how to deal with the issue. The main concern was for Gulf to stay in business in Angola.

Although the low demand for crude oil caused Gulf's profits to drop in 1975 (the year of political trouble and independence in Angola), the year before Gulf had pumped 54.6 million barrels from its Cabinda oil fields. During the transitional period MPLA denied any intention of nationalising Gulf;[35] therefore, in 1976, after the intense battles of the 1975 civil war, both the new People's Republic of Angola and Gulf were eager to restart production. By August that year, Gulf's Cabinda oil-fields were pumping out 123,000 barrels daily.[36]

There were other factors which began to shape the US approach to the Angola situation long before Andrew Young's pronouncements on the Angola issue. In spite of the big fuss in 1977 about the Cuban military presence in Angola, world opinion was already leaning favourably toward the MPLA government. 'By the 18th of February 1976, 73 nations had recognized the People's Republic of Angola (40 African, 18 European, 12 Asian and 3 Latin American). More countries followed suit in the ensuing weeks.'[37] By the time Young made his favourable comments about Angola, world opinion had already affected the US position on the Angola question. In 1977 Angola's diplomatic relations with Western nations did not seem to be under any strain; its greatest problems emanated from Zaire and South Africa.

In October 1975, when South African troops began to assist the rebel forces of the National Front for the Liberation of Angola (FNLA) and the National Union for Total Independence in Angola (UNITA) in the fight against the MPLA, the Soviet Union increased its arms supplies to Angola and Castro sent in Cuban troops. Thus it became clear to the US State Department that the military alliance between Angola and the Soviet Union and Cuba was a very strong one. The United States, just out of a war in Vietnam, did not want to be involved in a military crisis in Angola, nor did it need a confrontation with the Soviets over the Angola issue. It was clear that the MPLA was the best choice of the four liberation groups – the Front for the Liberation of the Enclave of Cabinda (FLEC), the FNLA, UNITA, and the MPLA. Since the other organisations were assisted by the unpopular South Africans, Soviet–Cuban support for Angola looked to be a progressive move.[38] Given the situation, it seemed that the United States would have to compete with the Soviet Union and Cuba for a positive image in the region of Southern Africa and this was a mission which called for such a character as Andrew Young.

The Carter Administration strategy toward Southern African issues was not original. It is very likely that Brzezinski, Carter and Young carefully studied the policy options which appeared in Kissinger's National Security Study Memorandum 39. But this is only speculation. Even if the Administration had not taken its strategies directly from Kissinger, its approach to Southern Africa amounted to a piecing-together of fragments from all the policy options which the Kissinger–Nixon and Kissinger–Ford State Department could not, or would not, adopt. At that time, US policy on Southern Africa seemed for the most part to follow option 2 of Kissinger's Memorandum 39. Here Kissinger suggests, 'Broader association with black and white states in an effort to encourage moderation in the white states, to enlist cooperation of the black states in reducing tensions and the likelihood of increasing cross–border violence, and to encourage improved relations among states in [the] area'.[39]

In the late 1970s an obvious manifestation of option 2 could be observed in US policy on South West Africa (Namibia). Rather than embark on direct negotiations with the South West African People's Organisation (SWAPO), the United States encouraged accomodation between SWAPO's enemy, South Africa, and the United Nations. This strategy could have been taken directly from the operational examples under option 2. The problem in Southwest Africa had arisen because 'At the end of World War I the League of Nations appointed South Africa as the Mandatory Power to administer the territory, but when the United Nations succeeded the League South Africa refused to accept its authority, and so subsequently the UN General Assembly voted in 1966 to terminate the Mandate.[40]

Kissinger's Memorandum contains five options, which together cover a vast range. The mixing-together of these options could well cause the kind of confusion that kept some of us wondering about the specifications of American policy toward Africa under the Carter Administration. In addition, Andrew Young as a popular figurehead further served the purpose of creating controversy and illusory notions about US foreign policy. Thus, Carter's Human Rights campaign was another controversial factor which overrode all others. Carter and Brzezinski's makeshift strategies for ideological manipulation were based on controversy contrived by the mass media and public perception of it. In the words of Zbigniew Brzezinski in his book *Between Two Ages* (1970), 'Persisting social crisis, the emergence of a charismatic personality and the exploitation of the mass media to obtain public confidence would be the stepping stone in the piece-meal transformation . . . into a highly controlled society' (p. 253).[41]

The controversy which surrounded Young and US foreign policy created the kind of climate which Brzezinski and Carter probably found to be tactically advantageous.

VIII ANDREW YOUNG THE MIDDLEMAN

Andrew Young has a way of talking about US foreign policy on the African liberation question which strikes us as interesting. In January 1977, in South Africa, Young said that the time was ripe for a non-violent change in South Africa via the 'market place.' He also said that this method of transformation was 'better than any other so-called revolutionary system going.'[42]

In line with the Trilateral Commission mandate, Young sees Africa as a potentially vital force in world affairs and as an important factor to the American politico–economic system. He also sees US investments in Africa as a move toward Africa's 'development'. The real point is that Young would, it seems, like Africa to remain a client of the West at almost any cost. To him this is a more stable arrangement.[43] Under clientage approach, the Western 'supermarket' can be used as a device of social, political and economic control.

In September 1979, Andrew Young led a delegation of twenty-two American businessmen[44] to Nigeria. This mission was a move toward consolidating the interests of Nigerian compradors and American 'big business'. The estimated value of the contracts negotiated was in the hundred millions. Though he denies it, it was alleged in the Nigerian press that Young personally negotiated a fertiliser deal for Pullman-Kellogg amounting to ₦333 million ($500 million). (₦ 1 = 1 Nigerian nairas. Note that the exchange rate of dollars to Naira fluctuates daily and may differ from year to year. In any case prior to 1979 the exchange rate used in this text is ₦1 to $1.8 or $1.87. In the course of this discussion the rate is as low as ₦1 to $1.5 from 1979 to 1982. At present the exchange rate is approximately ₦1 to $1.3.)

The Pullman-Kellogg contract became a controversial topic in the Nigerian press. The contract provides for a chemical-fertiliser plant which did not seem feasible to the critics of the deal. Nigeria is capable of providing organic fertiliser to its farmers through its cotton industry, which furnishes cotton hulls, and cattle farming in the Northern region, which provides manure. However, the greatest deterrent to efficient fertiliser industry in the country is its poor transportation system. Getting fertiliser to remote areas is virtually impossible at the present time. These and other observations perhaps caused the Pullman-Kellogg contract to be questioned in some circles of the new civilian government which assumed power shortly after Young's trade mission.

This trip to Nigeria was just one of the delegation's stops in Africa; it also visited Liberia, Senegal, the Ivory Coast, Cameroon, Cape Verde, Kenya, Tanzania and Uganda. The contracts negotiated during the mission grossed a total estimated at $1500 million – the same amount promised, but up to now only partially remitted, to Zimbabwe under the Lancaster House Agreement.

Although collaboration between ruling classes of the international bourgeoisie is hardly dependent on Andrew Young, Young did indeed use his influence for the further entrenchment of neocolonial economics, particularly in Africa and notably Nigeria. The September 1979 trade mission was the last official duty carried out by Young as US ambassador to the United Nations.

In October 1979, a few weeks after Young visited Nigeria, Washington's Star newspaper reported a breakthrough for some American firms in an article entitled 'Nigeria is Moving Capital Inland'. Some American firms were commissioned by the Nigerian government to perform consultancy services for the new capital city in Abuja. This was not the first time this had been announced in the United States. American imperialists considered this a breakthrough, because in the past the Nigerian construction market had traditionally been manipulated by British, West German and Italian companies.

Again, an article by Candido in the *New Nigerian* of 31 October 1979 reported that on 14 September the former Nigerian military government had lifted all national requirements for the DuPont Company. This special concession permitted DuPont to open offices without Nigerian partners (in contradiction to Young's speech before the Nigerian–American Chamber of Commerce) and provided for the lifting of other restrictions which were supposed to be strictly enforced. Actually the Nigerian government had invalidated its Indigenisation Decree. Moreover, the concession to DuPont was made without due legal process.

Allegations of unfair business practices were made against several transnational corporations in Nigeria, and the Voice of America African news service reported one such case. In August 1980 Gulf, Mobil and Royal Dutch Shell were asked to return 183 million barrels of oil to Nigeria on account of contract violations between 1975 and 1978. Nigeria charged the petroleum companies with breaches of production contracts. The value of the oil was estimated at $6000 million. The three oil companies denied the charges.

Some may ask, why shouldn't Africans want to increase business ties with the West? Why shouldn't Africa play the client role for whatever it's worth?

The clientage strategy is particularly counter-progressive in the African context because it creates economic ties that often allow the African entrepreneur to make a fast buck without improving public services or building up lasting independent primary industries. The usual pattern is that African states become markets for car-dealers, the subsidiaries of breweries, and appliance-dealers, hotel-owners and fertiliser-contractors. Though the Western demand for cheap labour had led to the opening of assembly plants throughout Africa, still there has been no significant industrial revolution in the black African states that allows total control of production – that is, from raw material to finished product. This in turn undermines the hope of eventual technological self-reliance.

Thus, when Western capitalists exploit cheap labour in Africa and the Third World, they actually contribute to the unemployment of the Western working class. It is ironic that people such as Andrew Young have supported the presence of such foreign manufacturers as International Harvester and General Electric in Africa when these companies have closed down plants in the United States, in many instances leaving Americans jobless.

The socio-psychological effects of the client relationship is that Africans do not have the necessary confidence to create a market for African-produced commodities in African communities – an attitude similar to that of the black Americans in considering the possibilities of black capitalism at the turn of the century. The very idea of locally produced commodities made from indigenous materials is threatening to the survival of the import market and the potential *nouveaux riches* in Africa. But, if anything is to be done about the selfish desire to make a fast buck without making any contribution to the hard task of nation-building, underdeveloped nations cannot afford the temptation of more get-rich-quick schemes.

As US ambassador to the United Nations, Andrew Young did not appeal ideologically to African governments concerned about building up collectively (socially) owned and locally controlled industries, although they shared certain pragmatic interests with him.

In spite of the fact that economists have said that on the whole Africa's dependency on the West has stagnated African development, middle- and upper-class Africans now talk of escalating economic contacts with transnational corporations. We also hear claims that imports and subsidiary agencies confront the indigenous entrepreneur with the kind of competition and international standards that provide the incentive and stimulus for the indigenous production of quality goods and services. As they see it, there is too much inefficient management and inferior production.

It sometimes seems that people believe that, before conceiving the idea of escalating business with the West, Africans had endeavoured to operate within a socio-economic mode isolated from the influence of Western capitalism – as if this new interest in the West were an alternative to something. The fact is that it is the selfish desire to get rich quick, to become cosmopolitan, to become clients and subsidiaries of Western capital – all this founded on warped notions about the relationship between the West and *development* – that is the real cause of inefficient management and inferior production in Africa.

While a successful plan for vast economic prosperity might be conceivable in America (though hardly as much as in the past), where industry, technology, various methods of appeasement and welfarism have enjoyed some 'success', in Africa only the semi-bourgeoisie is likely to benefit from an economic boom resulting from international trade. Reasons for holding such a view may not seem all that scientific to our opponents; however, historical observations in Nigeria, for instance, show very sharp class distinctions with heavy chauvinistic tendencies among the national ruling class.

Historically, in Africa the interests of the 'industrial' labour force, petty traders and peasantry are seldom considered with serious and sincere concern. The African ruling class has tended to resort to authoritarian and autocratic methods of social control, since it lacks the infrastructure capable of appeasement and welfarism on a broad base. Industrial unions and industrial action are suppressed by aggressive police forces, and the national revenue of most African states is expended in ways which are in the final analysis far more beneficial to the old indigenous capitalists and the *nouveaux riches* – some of whom invest their profits in property and small industries in Europe and America. What may appear to be a 'new deal' for American capitalists and the large American middle class, who see the mineral wealth of underdeveloped nations as a vital component of their economic productivity, may further widen the gap between rich and poor in Africa, and escalate tensions in African society. We must be aware of the internal class conflicts of African states and the dialectical connection between these conflicts and Western imperialism. This demonstrates that collusion between the African 'capitalist' and the Western imperialist has determined class conflicts on the continent.

In the case of socialist nations in Africa – for example, Ethiopia, Zimbabwe, Mozambique, Angola and Tanzania – critical analyses should be offered in the direction of explaining how far, quantitatively and qualitatively, the union of pragmatic socialism and Western capitalism has benefited, compromised or weakened the political will of black socialist nations. It should not be the case that in a developing socialist state, pragmatically tied to transnational capitalism, workers and farmers are continuously exploited, displaced and neglected, while state bureaucrats and other privileged elements in the ruling party wallow in luxury. In socialist Africa, as in the whole Africa, workers, peasants and the destitute ought to take first priority in socio-economic development since they constitute the most underprivileged sector of the society. There is no logical excuse why these desperate sectors should not immediately benefit from the 'growth' of technology and industry in socialist Africa. Modern socialism can not work without a highly productive industrial base; this is the motivating thought behind pragmatic socialism. But a pragmatic approach to realising socialism via the transnational corporate market needs to be assessed – and constantly reassessed – by the countries concerned with reference to the democratisation of national planning and the promotion of industrial self-reliance.[45]

Generally speaking, transnational corporations are not interested in African and Third World development. Rather their interest is primarily profit-oriented. Firestone's decision to sell its shares in Firestone Ghana Ltd (FGL) and Ghana Rubber Estate Ltd (GREL) is a case in point.[46]

After expressing its regrets over Firestone selling its 60 per cent share in these companies, the Ghanaian government saw fit to collaborate with OPIC, whose president was J. Bruce Llewellyn, the owner of Fedco Foods the black, Harlem-based enterprise. OPIC is underwriter for twenty promissory notes issued by the Ghanaian government to Firestone, representing an estimated 31 million cedis ($7.3 million).

According to a correspondent for West Africa magazine, the Firestone sale resulted from constraints on foreign-exchange allocations to the Ghanaian government, followed by a 50 per cent cut in FGL production, with a further 25 per cent cut expected. Thus in October 1980 Firestone decided to sell its shares.[47]

Understandably, the prevailing economic realities in Ghana would not permit the government to honour the promissory notes without external assistance, and OPIC agreed to delay submitting any of the notes to the Ghanaian government for six months.[48]

In spite of FGL's and GREL's grand expectations in 1967, by 1971 the two companies produced only 7.5 per cent of their projected production of tyres (300 tyres a day as opposed to a projected 4000). But, contrary to production figures, it was rumoured that the two Firestone-backed companies were draining Ghana of its rubber and foreign-exchange allocation.[49] In addition to official charges that

Firestone was depleting the government's foreign-exchange resources by using complex shipping methods, the University of Ghana, Legon, accused the company of 'exporting natural rubber far in excess of what was needed to purchase other raw materials such as carbon black, high tensile copper wire, nylon cord, etc'.[50] The President of Ghana, Hilla Limann, and a New York international business magazine made specific charges of unfair business dealings by Firestone and Valco, according to *West Africa*.[51]

Firestone's withdrawal from FGL and GREL provided an opportunity for the former black president of OPIC to play a positive role in the economic problems of an African country. However, the 'solution' adopted also indicates the status of black American 'leadership' in the international market. Certainly we can not compare twenty promissory notes valued at $7.3 million to the $500 million fertiliser contract between Nigeria and the Pullman–Kellogg Company.

Nevertheless, under a technical-management agreement, Firestone will offer managerial services to FGL and GREL. But, in addition to the costliness of this arrangement, Firestone can block its competitors from associations with persons in any way affiliated with FGL or GREL.[52]

The economic pressures affecting Ghana's rubber industry in 1980 and 1981 could not have come at a more awkward time. While Firestone was effecting its withdrawal from Ghana, the Ghanaian Parliament was considering an Investment Code Bill aimed at improving the investment climate in the country.[53] However, in learning that there is no social accountability in the international free-enterprise market, Ghana must now look to its most important resource, its people.

Notwithstanding the Ghana–Firestone case, perhaps the most vulgar example of the transnational corporations' lack of social accountability is their continued association with the racist white minority regime in South Africa. They have played an 'impressive' role in the economic and military development of apartheid, hence contributing to the hostile power relationship between blacks and whites in the Southern Africa region as a whole.

IX   ANDREW YOUNG AND THE PLO: THE CONFLICT
     BETWEEN BLACK AND JEWISH AMERICANS

When it came to the Arab–Israeli conflict, the Christian–liberal character of Andrew Young at times made him look politically naïve, to say the least. In one interview, Young drifted away from the political and diplomatic issues of the Arab–Israeli conflict and alluded to the common history and suffering of Christians and Jews. If we know anything at all about the Middle East crisis, Young's comparison of Christians and Jews was tactless for a US official. Though it was obvious that Israel's greatest supporter was the United States, in diplomatic circles the United States did not want to complicate matters by offending the Muslim members of the Organisation of Petroleum Exporting Countries (OPEC) and the United Nations by further fuelling ancient religious rivalries. Moreover, from a contemporary political standpoint; religion has no place in the Arab–Israeli conflict; the Middle East problem is a question of land rights and the rights of Palestinians to self-determination. These are the matters at stake.

In 1979 Young found himself on a 'Collision Course over the PLO'.[54] An unauthorised meeting between Young and PLO official, Zehdilabib Terzi, on 26 July 1979 subsequently caused Young and the US State Department much embarrassment by shaking the trust between Israel and the United States and by causing tension between black and Jewish Americans. This episode led finally to Young's resignation from his UN post.

Young's secret meeting with Terzi violated the US agreement with Israel that there would be no diplomatic meetings with the Palestine Liberation Organisation until the Palestinians accepted Israel's right to exist. The agreement supports UN Resolution 242. Since its adoption in 1967, Resolution 242 has always been rejected by the PLO because it indirectly acknowledges Israel's legitimacy without recognising Palestinian rights.

At any rate, the United States and Israel managed to keep faith between themselves despite Young's blunder.

As regards relations between black and Jewish Americans, Young's resignation embittered some black leaders who believed that it was conceded through pressure from the Jewish community. But what caused such a reaction? Why should black leaders be paranoid about Jews?

When it comes to the Arab–Israeli crisis, one often gets the feeling that many black Americans sympathise with the Arabs. A lot of black folk simply believe that it is wrong to take another man's land regardless of biblical history. At this juncture let us consider the general background of black–Jewish relations.

The black community and the Jewish community have always competed for sympathy from the Western world. Blacks have argued that the death of millions of slaves in the Middle Passage (trans-portation) and under slavery must deserve compensation. Through the media, Jews have used the Holocaust story to gain worldwide moral support and to justify their twentieth-century exodus to the Promised Land, Palestine. Yet, whereas they have succeeded in capturing the Promised Land with the help from the entire Western world, and enjoy marked economic success in the United States (with extensive control of the jewellery and fur industries, the mass media, and so on), black Americans, who have directly suffered under white-American domination, have received little recompense. Blacks believe Jews have received favours from the ruling class because of skin colour, since American Jews are after all European in origin and not the darker Asiatic type.

The success of Jews stems from their intellectual tradition and mercantilistic lifestyle, which has had direct effects on the black community in America. The general black public looks upon the Jewish petty-bourgeoisie with contempt because of their parasitic relationship with the black community. Jewish shop-owners have exploited generations of blacks, and, during the period of the 'mum and pop' (small, family owned) business, Jews rivalled black petty-capitalists, who had always sought to gain economic control over the black community.

There is also a religious clash between blacks and Jews. Black Americans, as Christians, disagree with Jews over the Messiah. There is some tension surrounding the fact that Jews do not accept Jesus as the God-sent Saviour. Also, there is the fact the Christians believe the Jews conspired to crucify Jesus.

In early 1970s a small delegation of black American Jews, called Hebrew Israelites, migrated to Israel, and discovered a hostile envi-ronment coloured by racism and embarrassment. This group of religious nationalists were denied the right to settle in the Jewish state which they believed themselves to be *religiously* tied to. This event received some publicity in the black press. The situation was seen for what it was – racist. This move by the Hebrew Israelites exploded into a black–white confrontation.

A great number of Jews in Israel have a European background and partly non-Semitic ancestry. These Jews, or better 'Zionists', migrated from Europe after the Second World War and 'centuries of exile'. In 1948 they seized state power over the former territory of Palestine. The dark indigenous Jews were displaced by the European Jews. Even as early as 1921, the Arabs of Palestine and Syria expressed their dissatisfaction to French cardinal DuBois regarding European Jewish colonisation.[55]

In the early seventies the black American Hebrew Israelites were making a similar exodus. Although the idea of black Judaism is not popular in the black American 'nation', the black press and nationalist scholar Yosef ben-Jochannan, author of *We the Black Jews* (1949), were of the attitude that black converts of Judaism should have as much claim to Israel as white Jewish colonisers.

This episode of black–Jew conflict also has class implications. While the Israeli regime rejected the Hebrew Israelite delegation, a perceived urban grass-roots cult, it is conceivable that Sammy Davis Jr, an entertainer, or Ray Tanter, a professor of political science at the University of Michigan, both members of the establishment and both black Jews, would be quite acceptable, since, in terms of productive relations, they have more in common with the Jewish artistic and intellectual bourgeoisie.

Although these details of black–Jew relations have had little impact on international diplomacy, they show what is at issue between blacks and Jews – though most people will not openly admit it.

With regard to the Andrew Young affair, the tension between blacks and Jews was immediately diffused because, unlike some black leaders, the black public at large was not really concerned about Jews. They saw Young's secret meeting with the PLO official as a State Department set-up, and Young's resignation as a convenient let-off for Carter. Young, however, refuted any accusation of foul play by Carter and at the time of his resignation encouraged black voters to re-elect Carter to the presidency in 1980.

The tension between black and Jews (as well as other American minorities), however, will intensify as the international economy changes and organisational resources in the United States become scarce. At the international level, Israel's relations with South Africa will no doubt be of concern to African-liberation advocates in America. Charges accusing Israel of being a supporter of apartheid have already been made, and we believe this will be one of the subjects of future black–Jew confrontations.

Israel was South Africa's fastest-growing foreign market in 1978. Exports from South Africa to Israel amounted to 400,000 tons of cargo. This included shipments of iron, steel, paper, timber, asbestos, canned goods, sugar, ferro-manganese and pesticides.[56] An estimated 'R650 [million] worth of South African diamonds go to Israeli cutters each year, but these do not appear in the [South Africa]–Israel trade figures'.[57]

Israeli exports to South Africa include potash, computers and other scientific and high-technology articles, paper products and base metals.[58] Industrial partnerships and foreign-exchange and taxation agreements have made for pleasant economic and diplomatic relations between Israel and South Africa. *Africa Contemporary Record* reports that 'Jack Rosmarin, chairman of the [South Africa]–Israel Chamber of Economic Relations, estimated that the total [South African] sales (including diamonds) to Israel would amount to no less than R[1000 million] a year in 1982 after the commencement of big coal shipments'.[59]

Black American advocates of the liberation of black South Africans from apartheid have been very critical of Israel's links with South Africa. In 1978, Andrew Young's second year as ambassador to the United Nations, South Africa and the United States were the only countries who increased their investments in Israel.

X AFTER THE RESIGNATION

It is understandable that, as an international socialite, Andrew Young would visit Nigeria quite often – especially in view of his shared visions with and fondness for General Obasanjo, the former Head of State and now agricultural entrepreneur; M. O. K. Abiola, the International Telephone and Telegraph Company (ITT) tycoon and former chairman of the ruling National Party of Nigeria; and Yur Adua, the rich and powerful Northern aristocrat and former military officer.[60] However, the motives behind some of his excursions after his resignation from the Carter Administration remain for the moment obscure, although they seem to have been informed by the diplomatic spirit which he demonstrated when in the United Nations.

Shortly after his resignation, early in 1980, Young met with Polisario guerrillas. The news-service agencies did not explain the purpose or nature of this meeting at the time, and no explanation has yet been forthcoming. In spite of the political controversy surrounding the Polisario movement, news agencies made Young's visit to a Polisario camp look like a pleasure trip.

Polisario has been demanding sovereign status for the area formerly known as the Spanish Sahara since 1975. At one point, after the Spanish had pulled out, Polisario was engaged in battle with foes to the north and south, Morocco and Mauritania respectively (the successor caretakers of the territory). Since 1978, when Mauritania withdrew its troops, the war has been waged against Morocco alone.

The US position on this territorial conflict encourages a settlement which exclusively recognises Morocco and underplays the Polisario liberation question. Morocco receives military (arms), economic and diplomatic support from the United States. It should be noted that the Moroccan government supports the UNITA rebels in Angola, and serves as a surrogate of the USA in this respect.

The most likely speculation about Young's meeting with the guerrillas is that he shared with them personal view about possible negotiations between Polisario and the Moroccan government. It is conceivable that Young sympathises with the Polisario cause. This speculation is grounded in the fact that some black middle-class groups, such as TransAfrica, support the Polisario campaign, just as they have sympathised with the PLO despite American foreign policy.

In late 1980 Young made a trip to Jamaica, where he campaigned for the re-election of Prime Minister Michael Manley. In this electoral contest Manley, a pseudo-socialist and Prime Minister for eight years, ran against a right-wing opponent, Edward Seaga, who defeated him. To most observers this was a contest between socialism and capitalism. The blazing contradiction underlying Young's support for Manley lies in the fact that for eight years, immediately prior to the elections, Manley's brand of 'socialism' had failed to cater for the well-being of the Jamaican masses, just as President Carter had failed to live up to his campaign promises to black Americans. Even though 'pragmatic socialism' had become the order of the day in Mozambique, Tanzania, Angola and Zimbabwe (each of which is willing to accept aid from capitalist countries, preferably 'with no strings attached'), the radical Marxists (the D. K. Duncan and Trevor Munroe factions), amongst Manley's supporters rejected that approach to national development. The persistence of proud and pure Marxism hurled the Jamaican people into economic turmoil, losing favour with the International Monetary Fund and the World Bank, with no national resources to fall back on.

Young enjoyed being a progressive politician, and the opinions he expressed on the situation in the Horn of Africa and in Angola and on the Wilmington Ten were to his credit in this respect. Nevertheless, his involvement in the 1980 elections in Jamaica was a reflection of his misinterpretation of that situation. Young gave his support to Manley as the candidate who had proven to be a political failure. The Jamaican people were already caught between the devil and the deep blue sea in that October election.

It appears that Young also has an interest in the labour movement in Africa. In February 1981 he showed up at the First Triennial Delegates' Conference of the Nigeria Labour Congress (NLC), in Kano, Nigeria. During the Conference a feud between NLC democrats and NLC 'Marxists' turned the proceedings into an ideological circus. The democrats at the Conference were primarily the David Ojeli (American Federation of Labour – Congress of Industrial Organisations) faction of the NLC, and the Marxists consisted of the Sunmonu union bosses, who guided the organisation for the first three years of its existence.

The implication is that Young attended the Conference to offer his support to the Ojeli AFL–CIO faction. Admittedly, there is no direct evidence for this: Young could swing either way. The Ojeli faction has a rather condescending attitude towards the working class, and this rendered it ineffective in the Conference election-proceedings. Its members lost every post they contested. The NLC 'Marxists' were able to retain Hassan Sunmonu as the principal leader of the NLC, although, from an ideological standpoint they are but a step above their 'democratic' opponents. They too have an AFL–CIO flavour about them and have steered the forty-two industrial unions of the NLC in the direction of economic unionism. They have failed to offer effective political education, and have based their struggle on economic demands, not political or genuinely revolutionary ones. Essentially, this group has failed to recognise that the seizure of state power is the fundamental task of working-class struggle.

As for the antagonism between democrats and 'Marxists' in the NLC, it should be noted that in theory there is no contradiction between democracy and Marxism. Marcel Liebman cites Lenin's disenchantment with the state's bureaucratic rule of the Soviet Republic, explicating the lack of democracy with reference to the perversion of his original vision:

> Writing in Pravda in March 1922, he called the bureaucrats 'our [the Soviets'] worst enemies'. . . . [They] gripped the entire Party and state [and persist doing so] and in a thousand and one ways eroded the ideal of October: *a Soviet democracy pledged to involve the humblest citizens – workers, peasants, soldiers, and housewives in political decisions, in the administration of public affairs, and the building of a new society.*[61]

The bureaucratic domination which Lenin speaks of here is indeed true in the case of the Nigerian Labour Congress, as well as the

Nigerian state as whole. And, in spite of the electoral systems of the United States and other Western nations, bureaucrats and elite elements also dominate the decision-making process in those societies. Despite all our hopes and fears, this is the dialectic and contradiction of social democracy – past and present.

It is unfortunate that the NLC Triennial Conference was saddled with factionalism; wherever it functions, the AFL–CIO is far from being a radically progressive organisation, and, as said earlier, the Sunmonu 'Marxists' of the NLC operate under a limited strategy of economic unionism. They have failed to challenge several labour laws and decrees of the Nigerian state which are explicitly anti-labour. If given ideological clarity, Nigeria's internal labour policy could make a real difference in her economic policy towards Western transnationals. But, while the NLC is an opposition organisation in rhetoric, it is also, technically, a wing of the Nigerian government (its sponsor), which is a client of Western imperialism.

2 The CIA: Covert Operations in Southern Africa, with Special Reference to Angola

A systematic study of the CIA's activities in Vietnam has revealed that covert operations are a decisive first step in military intervention.[1] For instance, the Gulf of Tonkin incident was precipitated by covert CIA operations. Throughout the sixteen years the United States was at war in Vietnam, the CIA waged a 'secret war' in Laos, hidden from the eyes of the American public. The assassination of Patrice Lumumba in the Congo (now Zaire) in January 1961 was the result of the CIA's massive covert operation directed against him.[2] The CIA's involvement in the assassination of Patrice Lumumba was revealed by a CIA officer who said he had 'an adventure in Lubumbashi, driving about town after curfew with Lumumba's body in the trunk of his car trying to decide what to do with it'.[3]

The aim here is to outline the overall structure and decision-making procedures of the CIA, and briefly to describe its approach in covert operations in Southern Africa and its links with the intelligence networks of the imperialist powers[4] and white minority regimes in the region. Finally, this chapter summarises the evidence and events relating to one major instance of CIA intervention – in Angola – to illustrate the possible patterns of covert US activities in Southern Africa, both now and in the future.

Covert activities are by definition the most carefully concealed intelligence operations. The most vital information about them comes to light, if at all, only after several years have elapsed. Extensive evidence now exists to show that the CIA's covert operations are now concentrated on Africa, especially Southern Africa as well as Central America and the Middle East.[5] In 1975 and 1976, the CIA's role in Angola hit the headlines. In 1978, John Stockwell, head of the CIA's Angola Task Force, published a book entitled *In Search of Enemies: A CIA Story*, which provides an in-depth picture of the CIA's intervention in Angola. This intervention took place despite Congressional approval of the Clark Amendment, which was later repealed in 1985.[6] The Amendment, passed in 1976, prohibited funding for covert activities in Angola and Zaire. Since its repeal in 1985, the Reagan administration has strengthened its ties with Jonas Savimbi and the UNITA rebels by promising ten to fifteen million dollars in military aid to that insurgency.

I STRUCTURE AND DECISION-MAKING PROCEDURES WITHIN THE CIA

CIA covert operations are sub-divided into two closely related functions: (1) intelligence gathering, mainly espionage; and (2) covert attempts to influence the internal affairs of other nations.[7] Espionage is particularly important in creating the groundwork for covert action. Since the early 1950s, the CIA's classic espionage techniques have been more effective in the developing nations than in the Soviet Union or China. Every CIA station in a developing country has developed an agent network, which sometimes includes the highest state officials, even presidents of countries.

CIA activities in Ecuador in 1961 exemplify the pattern.[8] With a total staff of twelve, the CIA station penetrated virtually every major political party in Ecuador. The President's personal physician and the chief of national police intelligence were CIA agents. Travel into and out of the country was closely watched. All diplomatic communications from Eastern Europe, the Soviet Union and China were monitored. Anti-communist youth movements were penetrated and funds were set aside for clandestine propaganda. Thus funds were provided for cultural activities and to pay the fares of young people to certain world gatherings so that they could speak out against communism. The CIA station in Ecuador also provided safe letter-drops for agent networks in Cuba. This was basically handled by the CIA base in Miami, Florida.

The development of a large number of local informants, known as 'assets' within the intelligence circle, allows the CIA to carry out a variety of functions.[9] First, the informants supply timely intelligence on the internal power balance. This gives the CIA a better chance of correctly predicting the local political situation. Secondly, these informants encourage an expansion of activities by indicating where and how operations can be mounted. Informants for small interventions can be recruited simply with money, but for bigger and more sensitive interventions covert assistance can be rendered directly by allies who have their own reasons and motivations for becoming directly involved.

Covert action is defined as

(1) Political advice and counsel;
(2) subsidies to an individual;
(3) financial support and technical assistance to political parties;
(4) support of private organisations, including labour unions, business firms, co-operatives and youth movements;
(5) covert propaganda;
(6) 'private' training of individuals and exchange of persons;
(7) economic operations;
(8) paramilitary or political operations designed to overthrow or to support a regime (such as the Angolan operation of 1975–6 or the US programmes in Laos).[10]

The operations typical of a CIA station in the developing countries include categories (1)–(7) above. These are known as 'low-level' operations, which usually occur simultaneously and overlap. Category (8) is a typical 'high-level' covert action – paramilitary and political action programmes are usually introduced where low-level covert operations have failed or do not exist.

The major difference between low– and high–level operations is that the latter seek to alter the internal power balance radically in the short-term, rather than merely influence it, as the former does. The assassination of Patrice Lumumba in 1961, the coups in Ghana in 1966, Chile in 1973 and Iran in 1953 are typical examples of high-level operations. Covert operations are very easy to introduce in developing countries for the following reasons: (1) government administration is weaker; (2) there is less security-consciousness; (3) there is apt to be more actual or potential diffusion of power among parties, localities, organisations and individuals outside the central government.[11]

Richard Bissell, head of the CIA's Clandestine Services from 1958 to 1962, pointed out that 'the impact of covert actions is increased if a comprehensive effort is undertaken with a number of separate operations designed to support and complement one another and to have a cumulatively significant effect'.[12] This operational integration may involve co-operation with other intelligence agencies, such as the national police intelligence agency of a particular country. Because of the CIA's development of a large and sophisticated apparatus for covert interventions, it is not surprising that the executive branch has made use of it in most crisis situations.

The command and control procedures for covert operations encourage the use of the CIA's violent option. The decision-making process for covert operations is highly secretive and elitist, and for this reason covert operations are vulnerable to abuse. CIA officials frequently encourage the escalation of covert activities, so pushing the US foreign-policy apparatus in the direction of high-level covert intervention.

In theory, the system of command and control over covert operations is tightly administered. The National Security Council monitored all CIA covert operations through a body known as the 40 Committee under the Nixon–Ford administrations, but renamed the Special Co-ordination Committee under the Carter Administration. Members of this committee usually include the Director of the Central Intelligence Agency, the National Security Adviser, the Chairman of the Joint Chiefs of Staff, the Deputy Secretary of Defense, the Under Secretary of State for Political Affairs, the Under Secretary of State for Policy Planning and other high executive officials. Despite the increased Congressional concern since the Clark Amendment of 1976, decision-making in this Special Committee is still limited to a small group of people.

The funds approved by the 40 Committee for covert-action projects from 1965 to 1975 fell into four major categories.[13] The largest category consumed 32 per cent of funds and involved projects providing some form of financial support for elections in foreign countries. The second category used 29 per cent of funds for news-media and propaganda projects. The third category, which accounted for 23 per cent, covered paramilitary and arms-transfer projects, including secret armies; financial support to groups engaged in hostilities; paramilitary training and advisers; and shipment of arms, ammunition and other military equipment. These were the most expensive projects. The fourth and the last category took up 16 per cent of the budget and financed a plethora of civic, religious, cultural, professional and labour organisations.

Proposals for covert action may be initiated at either the station or divisional level. From there they pass up the chain of command to the area division chief, the Director of Operations, the Director of Central Intelligence, and finally the National Security Council, which is the decision-making body.[14] This process strictly limits input from the

CIA's own Directorate of Intelligence, as well as from policy-making officials in other agencies, including the State and Defence departments. The use of special highly secret security clearances further restricts the number of participants in the decision-making process. Approval for covert-action proposals is practically routine. A former CIA official reported in the *Washington Post* that the 40 Committee was

> like a bunch of schoolboys. They would listen and their eyes would bulge out. I always used to say I could get $5 million out of the 40 Committee for a covert operation faster than I could get money for a typewriter out of the ordinary bureaucracy.[15]

The gathering of intelligence by the CIA through the Clandestine Services – i.e. through their local informants and their case officers in the field – further strengthens its urge to indulge in risk-taking activities.[16] For example, the failure of the Bay of Pigs operation in 1961 occurred because the CIA informants (the anti-Castro groups inside and outside Cuba and their case officers) wrongly insisted that Castro's control in Cuba was shaky.

All covert operations are designed to make it possible for the US President plausibly to deny involvement. He is usually informed of all covert operations, but he does not sign any documents approving or disapproving them. There are 'cover-ups' constructed to hide the US Government's involvements in all these operations. For instance, during the Angolan war in 1975–6, the CIA supplied the FNLA and UNITA with obsolete American weapons left over from the Second World War. Since such weapons are available everywhere in the world, the CIA felt their use in the Angolan war would not easily reveal US involvement in the conflict.

The CIA usually implements covert operations through area divisions and by creating special task forces. If a conflict arises the CIA may deal with it through a special task force created for the crisis in question. John Stockwell describes how

> In 1960, a small, quiet office handling several Central African countries suddenly became the Congo Task Force and then, as the Congo Crisis dragged on for years, the Congo Branch. The Cuban Task Force eventually became the Cuban Operation Group. The Libyan Task Force in 1973 faded almost as quickly as it was assembled. A task force supporting a serious paramilitary program would normally have a good Government Service (GS) 16 at its head, with a Senior

GS 15 as its deputy chief, and twenty-five to one hundred people on its staff, including half a dozen senior case officers to write the cables and memos, sit in on the endless planning sessions, and undertake the numerous individual missions that inevitably arose.[17]

The CIA can, with relative freedom, use about $50–100 million from the contingency fund at the disposal of the Director just to implement the early stages of a particular covert operation or possibly more at present.[18]

Morton Halperin, one of the most influential critics of the CIA, pointed out that the CIA's decision-making apparatus inevitably increases the chances that 'risky' operations will be chosen over more desirable alternatives; reduces the effectiveness with which the operations are designed and carried out; distorts decision-making within the executive branch in general; and lowers the quality of intelligence evaluation – supposedly the CIA's primary responsibility.[19]

II   CIA LINKS IN AFRICA

The Africa Division of the CIA's Clandestine Services is the smallest of all the area divisions. About 300–400 people are employed in it, based at the CIA headquarters in Langley, Virginia – a suburb of Washington, DC – or stationed in Africa. The smallness of the Division reinforces what John Stockwell refers to in his book as 'clubbishness'.[20]

Until the late 1950s, all clandestine operations concerning Africa were handled by the European and Middle Eastern divisions. The decolonisation of Africa in the 1960s motivated the CIA to consolidate and expand the newly created Africa Division. From 1969 to 1973, 'the number of CIA stations in Africa increased by 55.5 per cent'.[21] The main aim then was to stop communist advances through propaganda and political action. Intelligence operations were also directed at recruiting functionaries in the African socialist countries.[22] The first major CIA covert operation in Africa started in the Congo (now Zaire) in 1960.

CIA activities in Africa initially depended on liaison with the established intelligence services of the former colonial powers and the white racist regimes of Southern Africa. For example, the French intelligence service, the Service de Documentation Extérieure et de Contre-Espionage (SDECE) played, and is still playing, an important role in the internal politics of the former French colonies in Africa.[23] Relationships between the SDECE and the CIA were said to be difficult and sensitive during the presidency of Charles de Gaulle, but after his death the situation changed.[24] Former President Giscard d'Estaing's government initiated and encouraged a new era in US–French co-operation in covert operations in Africa, especially during the Angolan war. France supplied funds and paramilitary advisers for the FLEC.[25] Although the CIA usually informs the French of its activities, the SDECE does not usually reciprocate.[26]

A close liaison between the British intelligence agency, Military Intelligence-6 (MI6), and the US intelligence services has existed for many decades, especially over Southern Africa. This is the oldest and 'most important liaison operation of the CIA',[27] starting before the Second World War. The CIA has benefited from Commonwealth intelligence agreements fostered by MI6. MI6 has a series of working agreements with South Africa. As a result, the CIA has had very close contacts with South African intelligence services through a special agreement known as UKUSA (an acronym for the United Kingdom and the United States of America), as well as with the former white minority regime of Ian Smith in what is now Zimbabwe.[28]

In 1970, when the US Government wanted to close the US Consulate in Salisbury, the Director of the CIA, Richard Helms, was 'one of the strongest proponents of a pro-white policy in Africa'. Helms went to the extent of telling former President Richard Nixon,

> we do have useful and workable relationships in Salisbury [now Harare] with our counterparts there. I think it would be a shame to sacrifice those if we didn't have to . . . if we got rid of the consulate in Salisbury, we would have to run . . . operations out of some other context . . . I would like to see us keep a hand in there.[29]

The South African Bureau of State Security (BOSS) was created in 1968–9 and grew very rapidly between 1969 and 1975. Its budget increased by over 300 per cent during this period.[30] From its formation, BOSS sought to strengthen relations with other intelligence services. In July 1969, BOSS, the Rhodesian intelligence service and the Portuguese secret police held a week-long conference in Lisbon to discuss and map out strategies for collaboration in their war against the Southern African nationalist liberation movements.[31]

About the co-operation between BOSS and the CIA, John Stockwell said,

The CIA has traditionally sympathized with South Africa and enjoyed its liaison with BOSS. The two organizations share a violent antipathy toward communism and in the early sixties the South Africans had facilitated the agency's development of a mercenary army to suppress the Congo rebellion. BOSS, however, tolerates little clandestine nonsense inside the country and the CIA had always restricted its Pretoria Station's activity to maintaining the liaison with BOSS. That is, until 1974, when it yielded to intense pressures in Washington and expanded the Pretoria Station's responsibilities to include covert operations to gather intelligence about the South African nuclear project. In the Summer of 1975 BOSS rolled up this effort and quietly expelled those CIA personnel directly involved. The agency did not complain, as the effort was acknowledged to have been clumsy and obvious. The agency continued its cordial relationship with BOSS.[32]

The CIA and the South African regime co-operated closely in both the Congo and Angola, dealing with what they called their common enemy – Africans fighting against imperialist domination and for liberation.

Some Western authorities on CIA covert activities around the world have claimed that the CIA's self-imposed restrictions on operations inside white-ruled countries of Southern Africa led to its failure to predict the April 1974 coup d'état in Portugal.[33] In part, this failure was also associated with the CIA's close links with the Portuguese secret police, the Direccão Geral de Seguranca (DGS).[34] While the nationalist movements were growing in Africa in 1950s, the Portuguese secret police expanded their operations on the continent. Relations between the CIA and the DGS were developed during Allen Dulles's directorship of the CIA (1953–61) and many Portuguese intelligence officers were sent to the United States to be trained by the CIA.[35]

In 1962, under the Kennedy Administration, the CIA began to finance the FNLA, led by Holden Roberto. Roberto was pro-West and was regarded as a 'moderate' alternative to the Portuguese colonialists.[36] However, the Johnson Administration put a stop to this arrangement.

Under the National Security Study Memorandum 39, the Nixon Administration shifted further towards a conservative position and increased its support to the Portuguese and all the white-minority regimes in Southern Africa.[37] The CIA suspended major subsidies to

Roberto in 1969, and even closed down its stations in Mozambique and Angola owing to economic measures. It also reduced its personnel in Portugal itself, becoming almost entirely 'dependant upon the official Portuguese security service for information'.[38]

The CIA built up another highly controversial, secret liaison with the Israeli intelligence service, the Mossad, which seriously affected the African continent. The aim of Israeli foreign policy towards Africa was to develop a sophisticated foreign-aid programme for the newly independent African states, in an effort to end Israel's diplomatic isolation in the developing nations, and this presented the United States with an unprecedented opportunity to utilise the more 'favourable' image of Israel in the developing countries for her own ends.[39] The CIA handled its Israeli links through the counter-intelligence staff of Clandestine Services, directed by James Angleton.[40]

Beginning in 1969, the CIA started paying the Israelis 'millions' of dollars. These funds were 'regularly channelled to the Israeli's intelligence services for control and disbursement by the Prime Minister's office'.[41] The funding of Israeli's intelligence services by the CIA coincided with an expansion of Israeli military and paramilitary assistance to Africa. Most of this assistance went to Ethiopia, Tanzania, Uganda and Zaire.[42]

III THE CIA INTERVENTION IN ANGOLA

Following the downfall of the Portuguese regime in April 1974, events moved very rapidly in Angola, as rival political factions vied for power. Behind the scenes, representatives of South Africa and various Western powers used their ties with former agents of the Portuguese secret police, the DGS, to play an increasingly important role in an effort to influence the outcome of the conflict. About 12,000 DGS agents were very active inside Angola shortly before the 1974 coup.[43] Many of them had infiltrated African political groups, helping to create divisive trends.[44]

The CIA used its contacts with the DGS to strengthen the anti-MPLA forces. During Spinola's rule (April to September 1974), the overseas units of the DGS were not dismantled but reintegrated into the Portuguese Army, and in Angola these forces tried to weaken the MPLA. For example, on 14 September 1974, Spinola, Mobutu and the two reactionary Angolan nationalist groups, the FNLA and UNITA, discussed a settlement isolating MPLA. Spinola had underestimated the shift to the left in his own army, and was toppled a few weeks later. According to John Stockwell, the CIA's role in Angola at this early period was vague:

> In July 1974, the CIA began funding Roberto without 40 Committee approval, small amounts at first, but enough for word to get around that the CIA was dealing . . . into the race . . . During the fall of 1974 the CIA continued to fund Roberto, still without 40 Committee approval, and its intelligence reporting on Angola was predominantly from Zairean and FNLA sources.[45]

During summer and autumn 1974, the CIA formed the Portuguese Task Force to deal with the alarming events which had moved Portugal politically to the left.[46] Given the close relationship between the events in Portugal and Africa, it was speculated that the CIA's operations against 'communism' in both places were co-ordinated.

In autumn 1974, the French, through the SDECE, became 'more adventurous than any other Western Power'[47] in Angola. DGS officials based in Gabon supported the FLEC plan to seize Cabinda, the oil-rich Angolan province to the north, and facilitated the fleeing of nearly 1000 DGS-controlled flechas (strike troops) who joined the FLEC. French mercenaries such as Robert Denard and Jean Kay were involved in the creation of the FLEC military force.[48] Nevertheless, the attempted FLEC coup in November 1974 was aborted.

As the radical group within the Portuguese armed forces became stronger, the South African BOSS and the Rhodesian Special Branch police tried to preserve as much as possible the intelligence networks and paramilitary capability of the DGS.[49] Many DGS officials fled from Mozambique and Angola to Rhodesia and South Africa in summer and autumn 1974. A large number of the flechas left Mozambique for Zimbabwe and South Africa. Many of them joined the Rhodesian Selous Scouts, while others helped form anti-Frelimo groups in Mozambique under joint BOSS–Rhodesian control.

As already pointed out, on 7 July 1974 the CIA began to increase its covert funding of the FNLA, without 40 Committee approval.[50] On 26 January 1975, the 40 Committee officially approved $300,000 to fund the FNLA, marking the beginning of what was to develop into a $31 million CIA covert war in Angola.[51] In March 1975, the CIA reopened its Luanda station. From this station and those in Kinshasa (Zaire), Lusaka (Zambia) and Pretoria (South Africa), it supplied intelligence reports to the leaders of the Angola Task Force at the CIA headquarters in Washington, and, through it, to Secretary of State Henry Kissinger and other policy-makers.

It has been argued that the CIA's revived interest in Angola had 'infinitely greater significance than the US government has claimed'.[52] In monetary terms, the amount spent represented a thirty-fold increase on that approved by the US Senate Select Committee in November 1975 for the government's intelligence activities in Angola. CIA reports, apparently based solely on information from President Mobutu and Holden Roberto, suggested that the FNLA was militarily stronger than the MPLA or UNITA.[53] The expansion of US aid 'gave rise to speculation that the US was bent on trying to assure FNLA dominance'.[54] John Stockwell argued that

> the original 40 Committee options paper acknowledges the United States' vulnerability to charges of escalating the Angola conflict when it stated that a leak by an American official source would be serious, that we would be charged with responsibility for the spread of civil war in Angola.[55]

Furthermore, it was evident that increased US aid to the FNLA preceded the expansion of Soviet arms shipments to the MPLA, which only began in March 1975, almost two years after Soviet aid to Angola had been suspended.[56]

The conditions in Angola were clearly linked to events taking place in Portugal since the coup of April 1974. On 19 August 1975, the Portuguese Foreign Minister, Mario Soares, maintained in an interview with a German newspaper that he had engaged in negotiations with the African Independence Party of Guinea and Cape Verde (PAIGC) in Guinea-Bissau and Frelimo in Mozambique, but not with the liberation movements in Angola, because of the divisions between political groups and the mobilisation of conservative whites belonging to 'armies of mercenaries against the liberation movements'. He dismissed the possibility of a Rhodesian-style coup by white settlers in Angola, explaining that it could occur only if there were a 'rightist coup in the motherland [Portugal]'.[57] But, according to Soares, if the conservative 'solution' were not resisted, it 'would put in question the entire process of [Portuguese] decolonisation, [its] credibility and [its] goodwill'. Moreover, he argued, 'such a solution could facilitate the return of fascism to Portugal'.[58]

Unlike Soares, US officials viewed internal developments in Portugal and Southern Africa with growing alarm. Henry Kissinger voiced his opinion that Portugal was on the verge of a communist takeover. In September 1975 the 40 Committee met to consider possible actions by the CIA to counter what Kissinger called 'communist danger'.[59] In August, Lieutenant General Vernon Walters, the deputy director of the CIA, visited Portugal. Some critics of the CIA's 'dirty activities' insisted that the CIA was collaborating with right-wing elements in Portugal. In October, another CIA mission, including experts on currency problems and the Portuguese colonies, visited Portugal. When all these missions were visiting Portugal, Kissinger was advocating a policy of isolating Portugal in order to 'bring the leadership back to its senses'.[60]

The extent to which heightened CIA activity accounted for growing divisions in Angola, especially throughout 1975–6, is hard to determine. According to informed sources, throughout the period of the Angolan war the CIA Kinshasa station was said to have engaged in 'flagrant semi-overt activities', which 'ensured that American support to the FNLA would be widely known'.[61] The same sources claimed that these activities were carried out by the CIA in direct opposition to official Portuguese efforts to achieve a coalition to take up the reins of government in Angola. The CIA also ignored the view expressed by US diplomats in Luanda, that the MPLA was the best organised group and the most qualified to run the country.[62]

After the three main liberation movements in Angola (the MPLA, FNLA and UNITA) had started open warfare, the CIA stations and bases in Southern Africa were responsible for co-ordinating the distribution of US war material. On 17 July 1975, the 40 Committee met and authorised $14 million for further paramilitary operations inside Angola.[63] On 19 July, the first US C14 flight carrying arms to Angola delivered its cargo to the FNLA. Cargoes from CIA warehouses in Texas were assembled in South Carolina and delivered to Matadi, Zaire, on 12 September 1975 for collection by the FNLA.[64]

During a two-week reconnaissance trip to Angola, the CIA Task Force commander for that country, John Stockwell, met with both Holden Roberto, leader of the FNLA, and Jonas Savimbi, leader of UNITA, to discuss the progress of the war in order to plan strategies to guide future policy. After this trip, Stockwell, recommended that the US should either opt for a swift military victory via tactical air support and provision of advisers to the FNLA and UNITA, or should sharply de-escalate its involvement to a diplomatic level.[65] However, the Secretary of State, Henry Kissinger, had rejected a similar recommendation by the State Department.[66] On 9 December

1975, Kissinger acknowledged at a press conference that 'US aid to curb the success of the MPLA is being channeled through neighboring countries and some US allies (Zaire, Zambia, England and France)'.[67]

By the end of 1975, the CIA Angola Task Force consisted of the following five units: (1) an intelligence-gathering section; (2) a reporting section; (3) a paramilitary section; (4) a propaganda section; and (5) a supporting staff of assistants and secretaries.[68] John Stockwell pointed out that

> From the outset we [the United States] were deeply involved in managing the war from Washington, from Kinshasa, and from advance bases inside Angola . . . [the] intelligence effort was always subordinate to their [CIA officers'] advisory activities. CIA Communications Officers trained FNLA and UNITA technicians at the Angolan advance bases. Kinshasa cables reported that CIA paramilitary officers were training UNITA forces in Silva Porto and the FNLA in Ambriz . . . A retired Army Colonel was hired on contract and assigned full time to the FNLA command at Ambriz.[69]

The CIA propaganda section also had an important role. It was responsible for disseminating favourable articles to as many news sources as possible, so as to enhance FNLA support. CIA officers in Lusaka and Kinshasa submitted articles to local newspapers. If any of these articles were not picked up by international news agencies, they were transmitted via CIA cable to the Agency's other stations around the world, who saw to it that they were reprinted in the world press. For example, Reuters picked up a faked story from Lusaka which reported the capture of twenty Soviets and thirty-five Cuban advisers by UNITA forces.[70] The same story was carried by the *Washington Post* on 22 November 1975.[71]

Throughout the Angolan operation, the white-minority regime in South Africa was constantly informed of all developments by the CIA chief of station in Pretoria. It was reported that on two occasions the director of BOSS visited Washington and held secret meetings with the CIA's Chief of the Africa Division. John Stockwell explained that, 'without any memos being written at CIA head-quarters saying "Let's coordinate with the South Africans", coordination was effected at all CIA levels and the South Africans escalated their involvement in step with our own'.[72]

In September 1975, before Cuban military units landed in Angola, South African regular troops and armoured columns had penetrated deep into the southern provinces of Angola, in collaboration with UNITA forces. FNLA forces, aided by regular Zairean troops and mercenaries recruited with CIA assistance, attacked the MPLA forces in the northern provinces.[73] The MPLA forces with their loyal allies the Cubans began to push the invaders back on both fronts – in the south and in the north. By March 1976, the MPLA was victorious and in control of Angola.

If there is one issue that always unites all black African nations (regardless of how progressive) it is the apartheid policy of the white racist minority regime in South Africa. Almost all African nations bitterly opposed South Africa's invasion of Angola.[74] Thus the US Congress also rejected Henry Kissinger's request for open armed support for the FNLA and UNITA forces. The defeated South African forces withdrew in January 1976. After the MPLA's victory, South Africa claimed that the US government had covertly supported the invasion of Angola and had not kept her promises of overt assistance in the event of difficulties.

All the previous CIA covert interventions in Africa had been marked by ever-growing co-operation, direct or indirect, with the white minority regimes in Southern Africa, especially South Africa. Analysis of the CIA's high-level intervention in Angola helps one understand its probable present and future role in Southern Africa and in the continent of Africa as a whole.

All the evidence summarised in this section shows that the past US-sponsored covert operations in Africa have ranged from efforts to divide and disorient the Southern Africa liberation movements to circulation of false news to the local and international press. In addition we have tried to draw attention to the recruitment of mercenaries, encouragement of military coups and even assassination of leaders, all of which can be linked to the CIA and a 'closed door' American foreign policy. In carrying out these activities successive US administrations have apparently rarely, if ever, considered whether they were in fact assisting the group with the widest popular support. On the contrary, the sole aim of all these covert activities was to install or maintain regimes considered favourable to perceived US interests.

Early in 1980, the US Senate voted overwhelmingly to repeal the Hughes–Ryan Amendment,[75] which sought to restrict CIA covert activities in all parts of the world. Furthermore, on 24 June 1980 the

US Senate took the controversial step of attempting to lift restrictions on the US President that effectively prevented any US military aid and covert action to assist the UNITA forces that still continue to resist the MPLA government in Angola.[76] If the Senate action, sponsored by Senator Jesse Helms (Republican from North Carolina), had become law, it would have allowed the President to give military support to CIA covert action without making the action public and without an act of Congress specifically approving such aid. However, a compromise measure in which Senators Jacob Javits (Republican from New York) and Paul Tsongas (Democrat from Massachusetts) joined Senator Helms as co-sponsors was the one that was eventually passed. This amendment was attached to the 1981 Foreign Assistance Act. Under the Helms–Javits–Tsongas Amendment, if the President determined that US military aid for covert action was in the interests of national security, he could so inform the Senate Foreign Relations Committee and House of Representatives Foreign Affairs Committee behind closed doors.

The Senate action is a crucial first step in overturning the legal ban, instituted by the amendment to the Arms Export Control Act sponsored by Senator Dick Clark (Democrat from Iowa) in 1976, on CIA covert activities in Angola and Zaire. The Clark Amendment was passed overwhelmingly by both houses of Congress in 1976, reflecting Congressional fears that in the immediate post-Vietnam era the Ford Administration might involve the United States in the Angolan war.

The US Senate's repeal of the Hughes–Ryan Amendment and the passing of the Helms–Javits–Tsongas Amendment in support of US military aid for covert action are indications of the anti-communist mood in the US Congress. The author of the Helms–Javits–Tsongas Amendment, Senator Helms, described the current American mood as 'a new mood emerging in this country, of a spirit of reawakening to the dangers posed by the Soviets and their surrogates, as another sign of turning away from the earlier "overreactions" to the alleged abuses of covert action'.[77]

Based on this analysis, with the facts set out above, and the 1985 repeal of the Clark Amendment, CIA covert activities will be encouraged and will continue to increase in Southern Africa for the remainder of the 1980s.

3 The Carter Administration's Policy in Southern Africa, 1977–80

In 1969, Henry Kissinger, then President Nixon's National Security Adviser, commissioned a study of policy in Southern Africa. The result was National Security Study Memorandum no. 39,[1] which outlined five possible policy options for the Nixon Administration. Kissinger, in his capacity as National Security Adviser, recommended, and the Administration adopted, option 2, which stated,

> The whites of Southern Africa were there to stay, and the only way constructive change can come about is through them. There is no hope for the blacks to gain the political rights they seek through violence, which will only lead to chaos and increased opportunities for the Communists.[2]

The Nixon Administration built its entire Southern Africa policy on this option, which called for continuing of the rhetoric of the Kennedy and Johnson administrations, and maintaining 'public opposition to racial repression but relax[ing] political isolation and economic restrictions on the white states'.[3] This strategy also called for 'diplomatic steps to convince the black states of the Southern Africa Sub-region that their current liberation and majority rule aspirations in the area are not attainable by violence and that hope for a peaceful and prosperous future lies in closer relations with the white-dominated states'.[4] The Nixon Administration was going all out to deny the existence of the liberation movements in Southern Africa.

In reality, this policy choice was based on practical considerations, and not on moral considerations or on concern for human rights and fundamental democratic principles. Therefore, in the view of US officials, the Kissinger policy toward African aspirations for majority rule in Southern Africa represented a shift toward the white-minority regimes.

Kissinger involved himself in a whirlwind attempt to find solutions to the Zimbabwe constitutional crisis towards the end of the Ford (Republican) Administration, but it can hardly be said that at any time in the 1960s or early 1970s the United States had an effective African policy. Still, the African continent remained at the bottom of the State Department's agenda and the attitude in Washington was to leave African affairs to its two major European allies with major African interests, Britain and France.

After the inauguration of Jimmy Carter as President in January 1977, there were a few changes which, if hardly momentous, showed a more steady and sustained Washington approach to Africa, although the United States was still far too prone to cold-war attitudes to pursue a policy which stood up to pressures as they occurred. Accordingly, this discussion sets out to examine the Carter Administration's policy on Southern Africa between 1977 and 1980, and to indicate the possible patterns of current and future US policy in the context of the Southern Africa crisis.

The Carter Administration wanted to put a clear distance between itself and the Nixon–Ford administrations' policy on Southern Africa. Ambassador Andrew Young, who was President Carter's 'point man' (leading spokesman) on an as-yet unformulated Southern Africa policy, criticised the Nixon–Ford administrations for looking at Southern Africa from the point of view of the cold war in Europe. In place of Kissinger's policy, Young advocated one that would moderately try to accommodate, at minimal cost to the Western capitalist system, the African demands for majority rule in Southern Africa.

Ambassador Young drew on his Civil Rights experiences of the 1960s to develop a strategy for the Carter Administration's Southern Africa policy in early 1977. The Young strategy we here refer to as the 'Atlanta model'. Young based it on Martin Luther King Jr's non-violent approach in enlisting the support of white American liberals and business folk in putting an end to racial segregation in the Southern states in the 1960s. A part of the 'Atlanta model' was the Carter Administration's strategy of putting pressure on the illegal white-minority regimes of Southern Africa through the US and South African business communities. In an interview with the South African *Financial Mail* on November 1976, President-elect Jimmy Carter said,

I think our American businessmen can be a constructive force in achieving racial justice within South Africa. I think the weight of our investment there, the value the South Africans place on access to American capital and technology can be used as a positive force in settling regional problems.[5]

Young also warned that, for the United States to avoid political and economic chaos in Southern Africa, the Carter Administration had to recognise the African leadership in both Angola and Mozambique. In a testimony before the House of Representatives International Relations Committee, Young warned that, regardless of their political belief in socialism or Marxism–Leninism, presidents Agostinho Neto of Angola and Samora Machel of Mozambique were men educated in Western and Christian traditions. He warned that, if the United States refused to deal with them, there were young African nationalists in Southern Africa who were more radical and not educated in Western Christian traditions. If any of these came to power, it would most likely mean instability and chaos for economic interests in Southern Africa. As a departure from the Nixon–Ford policy, Young advocated that the Carter Administration should talk with the independent African states and the white racist regimes and start a direct dialogue with the nationalist groups in Southern Africa.[6]

President Carter's first Secretary of State, Cyrus Vance, emphasised the Administration's Human Rights policy as far as Southern Africa was concerned. This emphasis has been attributed to a policy disagreement within the State Department, where Secretary Vance's Human Rights approach was opposed by Zbigniew Brzezinski's cold-war stance in relation to Southern Africa issues.[7] To justify his position and the approach he thought the Carter Administration should follow in Africa, especially concerning the Southern Africa conflict, Vance said,

> Our policies must reflect our national values. Our deep belief in human rights – political, economic, and social – leads us to policies that support their promotion throughout Africa. This means concern for individuals whose rights are threatened – anywhere on the continent. And it means making our best effort peacefully to promote racial justice in Southern African nations who, having won their freedom, are determined that all of Africa shall be free.[8]

He went on to say, the most effective policies toward Africa are affirmative policies. They should not be reactive to what other powers do, nor to crises as they arise. A negative, reactive American policy that seeks only to oppose Soviet or Cuban involvement in Africa would be both dangerous and futile.[9]

At the beginning of the Carter Administration, the economic disruption caused by warfare in Southern Africa was seen to pose a grave threat to the Western world. Nevertheless, while the Carter White House was indeed concerned about Soviet involvement in Southern Africa, it appeared to feel that the best way to contain the Soviets' influence was through an orderly, non-violent transfer of political power from the white-minority regimes to democratically elected governments. The Carter Administration felt that such orderly transfer of power favoured the West, while escalating warfare by the liberation movements favoured the Soviets. African leaders were pleased by Carter's disregard of the Kissinger–Ford view that communism and the Soviet Union were the only threats to Western interests in Southern Africa.

Initially, the Carter Administration did not seem disturbed by pleas from the white-minority regimes of Ian Smith and John Vorster that an orderly transfer to majority rule without guarantees of a Muzorewa-type controlled African leadership would mean a Soviet takeover of the economic resources of Southern Africa. Ambassador Young attached little weight to the economic threat that radical and progressive African leadership could pose for Western interests in Southern Africa, and gave Angola as a practical example. He pointed out that, while the Soviet Union had given over $400 million in military assistance to the MPLA government, the US firm Gulf Oil exploited the crude oil from Cabinda province of Angola.[10]

From the moment the Carter Administration entered the White House in January 1977, the United States began improving its relations with African countries, attempting by direct dialogue to find peaceful solutions to the Rhodesian conflict[11] and the Namibian independence problem.

President Carter sent his vice-president, Walter Mondale, to meet with the South African Prime Minister, John Vorster, in Vienna in May 1977.[12] Carter instructed Mondale to tell Vorster that relations between their two countries would depend upon how positively South Africa moved towards democracy at home. During this meeting Mondale made it clear to the South African Prime Minister that the white-minority regime should make way for full political participation of black South Africans. He said, 'every citizen should have the right to vote and every vote should be equally weighed'.[13]

Young, as US ambassador to the United Nations, was particularly instrumental in improving American relations with the African continent. During his fact-finding trip to Nigeria and Southern Africa in February 1977, he met and assured the Nigerian leaders, the 'front-line', presidents and the leaders of the Southern Africa liberation movements – the Patriotic Front (ZANU–ZAPU), SWAPO and the African National Congress of South Africa (ANC) – that the Carter Administration was prepared to work on their behalf, and support them, in their aspirations for African majority rule.[14]

In pursuit of the Administration's strategy for South Africa, the US government later took the lead in trying to bring about a peaceful transition to majority rule in Namibia. The Contact Group of five Western nations (the United States, Britain, France, Western Germany and Canada), working under the auspices of the United Nations, set out to exert pressure upon the South African government to grant independence to Namibia. The United States, as the most powerful Western nation, was the one that could exert the most pressure, and, in co-operation with the other four Western governments, it submitted proposals to SWAPO and South Africa aimed at bringing an end to the war in Namibia. The Contact Group's proposals were as follows.

(1) A special representative of the UN Secretary-General should be appointed in order to satisfy himself of the fairness and appropriateness of the political process leading to 'free election' for a constitutional assembly. Control and administration of the electoral process would, however, rest with the South African Administrator General.
(2) There should be a phased withdrawal of South African troops over a three-month period, leaving only 1500 troops, who would stay in two northern bases until after the elections.
(3) There should be a further attempt to settle the question of who owns Walvis Bay, South Africa or Namibia.

The Western plan was vague on a number of key points, including the strength of the proposed UN forces.[15] It was proposed that the Walvis Bay question be left out, to be solved after Namibian independence.

The Carter Administration's plan for a peaceful transition to majority rule in Namibia seemed for a brief period to be on the road to success, until South Africa launched an invasion of Angola and attacked a SWAPO camp 150 miles inside Angola. According to

SWAPO sources, the South African troops killed over a thousand people in that attack, about 300 of whom were women and children. SWAPO then rejected the Western proposals, and was only persuaded to reopen negotiations with the help of the frontline states. However, since early 1978 South African troops have launched many attacks on SWAPO bases inside Angola, killing and maiming thousands of freedom fighters, women and children. Hence, in December of the same year, a rigged election staged in Namibia produced what was claimed to be a victory for the Democratic Turnhalle Alliance (an anti-SWAPO group set up on Pretoria's orders) and a defeat for SWAPO. All the efforts of the United Nations and the Contact Group to get South Africa to accept the UN plan failed in 1979. Efforts to negotiate a peaceful settlement in Namibia were resumed in October 1980, and discussions held in Pretoria, South Africa. Both South Africa and SWAPO agreed in principle to an all-party conference to be held in Geneva early in January 1981.[16]

From early 1978, a decided shift became apparent in the Carter Administration's policy on Southern Africa. The initial emphasis on a peaceful transition to majority rule gave way to a revival of East–West confrontation politics in Africa. Instead of focusing on putting an end to minority rule in Southern Africa, the Administration began to contrive anti-Soviet and anti-Cuban statements. A report in the *Washington Post* commented, 'White-House strategists for at least two months have attempted to funnel sophisticated arms and funds clandestinely to African guerrilla forces fighting Soviet-backed Cuban troops in Angola'.[17] The report further stated that Presidential Security Adviser Zbigniew Brzezinski argued that this was one way in which the United States would 'pin down the Cubans' and limit their role in Africa. Thus, aid was to be funnelled through an unnamed third party, likely to be South Africa.[18] Brzezinski's argument was incongruent with the philosophy expressed in the Clark Amendment, and in fact represented a continuation of the Kissinger strategy.

As a direct consequence of the new cold-war approach of the United States, it became unclear whether any of the Carter Administration's previous Southern Africa policies and strategies remained operative. It was no longer certain that it would continue to support the September 1977 Anglo-American Proposals for a peaceful settlement in Zimbabwe.[19] It seemed that the Carter White House was increasingly moving towards accepting some version of Ian Smith's so-called 'internal settlement', negotiated by Bishop Abel Muzorewa, the Revd Ndabaningi Sithole and Chief Jeremiah Chirau in

March 1978. The United States was looking for a way to persuade Joshua Nkomo, leader of ZAPU and co-leader of the Patriotic Front, to join the so-called internal settlement. When we interviewed him in Washington on 18 June 1978, Nkomo categorically rejected the 'internal settlement' and condemned the US government's increasingly vigorous anti-Cuban campaign.[20]

The US government's concern to involve Nkomo in the internal settlement, lending it greater credibility, stemmed from its belief, for historical reasons, that he was moderate and pro-West, and from its hope that, by supporting Nkomo it would prevent Robert Mugabe, leader of ZANU and also co-leader of the Patriotic Front, from gaining power. Mugabe was perceived as a Marxist, and likely to subject the colonial political economy to a radical restructuring.

The emergence and eventual success of the Patriotic Front (with Mugabe elected the first Prime Minister of a free Zimbabwe) was the achievement, first, of the Patriotic Liberation Army, jointly led by Nkomo and Mugabe; secondly, of the frontline states (Tanzania, Zambia, Mozambique, Botswana and Angola); thirdly, of the Commonwealth of Nations; and fourthly, of the British government – but hardly of the US government.[21]

Late in 1977, certain elements in the Carter Administration's strategy began to indicate a more explicit desire to destabilise and destroy the MPLA-led Angolan government, the Administration considered hostile to Western interests in Southern Africa. In May 1978, the CIA Director, Admiral Stansfield Turner, and his Africa Division chief, James Potts, approached Senator Dick Clark (author of the previously mentioned Clark Amendment, which decreed that direct or indirect US aid to any nation planning military action in Angola must receive explicit Congressional approval) with a proposal to heat up the Angolan conflict as a means of causing problems in Southern Africa. According to John Stockwell, 'Apparently only Clark's refusal to cooperate, stopped us [the United States] from generating yet another Third World tragedy.'[22]

The growing anti-communist attitude within the Carter Administration, and the continued application of anti-communist criteria for intervention in Southern Africa, seemed to justify the belief that the United States could conceivably intervene militarily on the side of the white-minority regime of South Africa. During the war between Ethiopia and Somalia over the Ogaden region in 1977, Brzezinski said, 'The problem isn't the war, the problem is the Soviet and Cuban presence',[23] this attitude then pervaded every Carter Adiministration policy, strategy and programme for Africa, especially Southern Africa. Brzezinski could easily claim that the problem in Southern Africa was not apartheid or white-minority rule, but rather the Cuban and Russian presence in Angola, Soviet assistance to SWAPO in Namibia or the ANC in South Africa, and the alleged Cuban presence in Tanzania, Zambia and Mozambique.[24]

Whereas earlier in 1977 the Administration had seemed to view South Africa as a Western outcast, later it came more and more to view it as a Western outpost. Logically, the Administration's new cold-war stance drew South Africa and the Western nations into close military co-operation with each other. Despite the US vote for the UN mandatory arms embargo against South Africa on 4 November 1977, it began to appear that the apartheid regime in South Africa would be looked upon by the United States as a strong ally in its fight against Soviet and Cuban influence in Southern Africa. Brzezinski's predecessor in the White House, Henry Kissinger, had after all used the same argument to encourage and fund a CIA paramilitary operation in Angola between 1975 and 1976.[25]

The voices criticising US intervention in Angola were decreasing and growing weaker, and a number of influential private American organisations had begun promoting the cause of the UNITA rebel forces in Angola. One such organisation, the conservative, New York based Freedom House, sponsored UNITA leader Jonas Savimbi's American tour in November 1979. During his trip he met with many American leaders, including former Secretary of State Henry Kissinger, Senator Henry Jackson, Senator Daniel Moynihan and labour-leader Lane Kirkland.[26]

According to American press reports, the purpose of Savimbi's trip was to abort possible US recognition of the MPLA government in Angola. The United States is the only Western government which does not have diplomatic relations with Luanda. And, since the resignation of Andrew Young as US Ambassador to the United Nations, and of Cyrus Vance as Secretary of State, State Department opposition to the arming of the Savimbi forces has seriously deteriorated and weakened.

In June 1980, South Africa boasted that its military attacks on Namibian liberation camps based in Angola were its greatest feat since the Second World War, and the response from the United States was silence. There were no urgent calls for meetings of the UN Security Council, as on the American invasion of Cambodia in 1970, or the Soviet invasion of Afghanistan in December 1979.[27] The

Human Rights voices of the Carter Administration were silent in the wake of forty-two killed and over 200 wounded, all innocent Namibians and Angolans. And it all happened inside Angola within one month.[28]

In the early days of the Carter Administration, the influence of area strategists on US policy on Africa was obvious in the efforts negotiate a peaceful settlement and African majority rule in Zimbabwe. In brief, the area strategists focused first and sometimes exclusively on the local causes behind conflicts, such as national, racial or religious factors. They counselled against US involvement in any conflict simply as a reaction to the Soviet Union's active participation. The global strategists, on the other hand, generally focused first, and sometimes exclusively, on the ramifications (the spill-over effects) of the conflicts for overall East–West super-power relations. If the Soviets were thought to be acting against Western interests, then the globalists (Brzezinski types) argued, the United States should support a competing side or withhold its co-operation in some other area of special interest to get an edge over the Soviet Union.

Brzezinski, in his capacity as President Carter's National Security Adviser, turned to 'linkage politics'. This [29] meant that, if the Soviets or Cubans made trouble in one area of the world – as in the Soviet invasion of Afghanistan, the United States would seek to punish the Soviets by denying them something in another area – for instance, by refusing to ratify the Strategic Arms Limitation Treaty (SALT). The linkage approach was cherished by the Nixon Administration.[30] When it was applied in US foreign policy in South-East Asia it had little or no effect. The Carter Administration in 1977 began by disowning Nixon's linkage politics, but after the conflicts of 1977 and 1978 in the Shaba province of Zaire, between the Katangese and President Mobutu, and the war between Ethiopia and Somalia over the Ogaden region in 1977, the Administration appeared to be sliding toward the linkage approach in its policy on Southern Africa. Apparently the Carter White House could not work out any way of reacting to Soviet and Cuban support for the Southern Africa liberation movements other than the Nixon strategy which Carter himself had initially condemned.

The new amendment co-sponsored by Senators Helms, Javits and Tsongas in June 1980, concerning the CIA (see the previous chapter), was strongly opposed by the State Department's African Bureau, the TransAfrica organisation, and some other black organisations, along with concerned African scholars and many Africanists in the United States. In the first place, these elements saw that, if the Amendment were passed by Congress, it would raise serious political problems for the United States in Africa in the 1980s and tarnish the image of President Carter for African leaders, who regarded him as a moralist president. Carter had said publicly that the United States had no intention of getting involved in Angola, and White House officials claimed that this was a standing policy. Secondly, the Amendment was proposed at a time when relations between Angola and the United States seemed to be improving and there seemed to be some hope of progress in negotiations on the independence of Namibia, a debate in which the MPLA government in Angola has been playing a key role since late 1978. Thirdly, the Amendment promised to damage the image of the United States with newly independent Zimbabwe, and obstruct the chances of a good and close relationship between the two countries. Fourthly, if Congress passed the Amendment and Carter resumed military aid to the white regime in South Africa and to the UNITA rebels in southern Angola, and generally supported covert activities in Southern Africa in the 1980s, the Western Contact Group led by the United States and working with South Africa for a peaceful transition to independence in Namibia would lose the co-operation of the MPLA government in Angola and the other frontline states. It would also encourage the South African liberation movement led by the ANC and the Pan-African Congress (PAC), to intensify the war for liberation, resulting in a terrible bloodbath inside the Republic of South Africa in the 1980s.

Finally, a close look at the Carter Administration's Southern Africa policy from 1977 to 1980, and the policy now being advocated by its successor, the Reagan Administration, suggests that, although the change towards a more interventionist US policy on Southern Africa will accelerate in the 1980s, policy shifts will be subtle and differ more in style than in substance.

4 Nigeria, South Africa and the US Connection: Myth and the Western-Proclaimed 'Giant of Africa'

Severe strains in Nigeria's relations with the United States occurred during the first year (1976) of the Mohammed–Obasanjo regime. The central issue was Angola. Nigeria's perception of the Angolan conflict was fundamentally opposed to that of the United States. Hence, the action which Nigeria took to help effect a settlement ran counter to actions taken by the United States. Although open support for the MPLA would have been the most progressive move, Nigeria's initial position was to encourage the three Angolan groups – the MPLA, FNLA and UNITA – to seek some form of mutual accommodation: to agree on a government of national unity and to work together for the benefit of their people. Nigeria was even prepared to support some delay in the transfer of power in order to achieve the policy goals of securing independence through a government of national unity in Angola. Foreign intervention in Angola completely changed the situation and necessitated an immediate review of Nigeria's policy on Angola. Nigerian leaders believed that a truly independent Angola could neutralise the Caprivi Strip and deprive South Africa and the Ian Smith regime in Rhodesia of their military base there, which they used to frustrate the support of Zambia and Botswana for liberation fighters in the area. Because of its strategic and economic interests in South Africa, the United States perceived Angola more or less from the South African standpoint. That is, the United States wanted a government in Angola which would neither threaten Western interests in Southern Africa nor seek to force radical political changes in the region. The United States supported the FNLA–UNITA alliance, which was backed by South Africa, and overlooking South

72

Africa's military intervention in the Angola conflict, concentrated criticisms on the involvement of Soviet and Cuban forces on the side of the MPLA.

It is against this background that the present chapter aims to examine and analyse the connection between Nigeria, South Africa, and the United States between 1975 and 1979 – that is, from the period of the Angolan civil war in 1975 up till the Lancaster House independence talks on Zimbabwe in 1979.

As pointed out earlier, Nigeria initially did not take sides in the Angola conflict. It did not approve of Soviet and Cuban military involvement in support of the MPLA because all forms of foreign intervention were seen as obstacles to the formation of a government of national unity. This is all the more understandable in that Nigeria itself is a peripheral capitalist state. Nevertheless, it did understand that Soviet aid to the MPLA predated Angola's independence, that the MPLA's armed struggle against Portuguese colonialism was made possible by continued Soviet assistance in terms of money, equipment and men, and that the Cubans were not out to colonise Angola, seize its wealth and frustrate the total liberation of Southern Africa. According to a reliable source, it was claimed that, during a trip to East Africa to explore what contribution the Nigerian government could make in the effort to reconcile the three warring nationalist factions in Angola, the Nigerian Commissioner for External Affairs, retired Major General J. N. Garba, 'suggested, publicly, that Portugal should postpone Angolan independence to avoid the impending civil war and chaos'.[1]

The change in Nigeria's policy on Angola came about for the following reasons.

(1) South Africa sent an invasion force into Angola, and planned to overrun the most patriotic of the Angolan liberation movements, – the MPLA – and install in power the puppet reactionary groups, the FNLA and UNITA.

(2) The Western economic interests which exploited Angola during colonial times sought 'to continue to avail themselves of Angola's wealth to their selfish advantage and to the detriment of Angolan peoples even after their independence'.[2]

(3) While the US government put pressure on the Nigerian government to maintain its neutrality, Nigerians, on the other hand, both within and outside government, wanted to throw the Administration's weight behind the MPLA.

Nigeria therefore decided to support the independence of Angola, recognising the MPLA as the legitimate government of Angola, and assisting it in its struggle to unify the country and defeat the South African invaders and collaborators. It also decided to approve Soviet and Cuban involvement on the side of the MPLA as legitimately requested by Angola and unlikely to undermine the country's independence. Nigeria not only recognised the MPLA: it gave ₦13.5 million (about $24.3 million) and military supplies to the MPLA government and launched a diplomatic offensive among African states to get them to recognise the MPLA.[3] The fact that, by February 1976, seventy three nations (forty African) had officially recognised the MPLA government, made Nigeria's new attitude hardly original.

The Ford Administration in the United States went all out to fight what it perceived as the dangers of communism and the export of Cuba's revolution into Southern Africa through Angola. President Ford wrote personal letters to African heads of states, and, along with his Secretary of State, sent a high-powered diplomatic mission to OAU governments to explain US policy on Angola. The overall objective was to dissuade other African governments from following in Nigeria's footsteps, and to urge OAU member states that had recognised the MPLA to change their policy position. American leaders used every available opportunity to warn Africa and the international community at large that they wanted the Soviet Union and Cuba out of Angola, and did not favour the MPLA government. Nigeria replied angrily to President Ford's letter and made its anger public by cancelling a scheduled visit of Secretary of State Henry Kissinger to Nigeria. This was the climax of a series of events marking a worsening of relations between Nigeria and the United States, the first having been the Nigerian government's takeover of the US Information Service buildings and radio-monitoring stations in Lagos and Kaduna respectively. Ford's message to the OAU, and particularly to Nigeria, was described as 'Ford's overbearing directive'.[4]

Indeed, at the beginning of the Mohammed–Obasanjo regime, a deliberate choice was made to adopt a more militant and radical strategy in support of the liberation cause in Southern Africa. The Nigerian government assisted the liberation movements in every way possible. For example, on assumption of office in July 1975, General Mohammed allowed some of these groups to open up offices in Nigeria – a departure from the traditional government policy. In fact, the government adopted an open-door policy for African exiles from areas in which the liberation wars were being fought. Though it experienced difficulties and frustrations, the Mohammed–Obasanjo regime did not cease giving financial as well as moral assistance to the liberation movements – a practice which had started during Gowon's era. Indeed, the financial aid was increased, so as to encourage other OAU states to participate in the liberation efforts.

For instance, in September 1975, the Federal government of Nigeria gave ₦17,400 ($32,750) to the African National Congress (ANC) of Zimbabwe, 'for appropriate use in the interest of all the people of Zimbabwe'.[5] This sum was given to Bishop Abel Muzorewa just after the announcement that Joshua Nkomo was leaving the ANC. Though appreciative of the Nigerian government's gesture, Muzorewa said that this was the first time Nigeria had provided funds directly. He also appreciated Nigeria's provision of many places in its universities and schools for Zimbabwean students. It was in the following month that Garba publicly confirmed Nigeria's recognition and support for the ANC under Muzorewa.[6] This, however, is indicative of Nigeria's misconception of the factions in Zimbabwe since Nkomo's break from ANC was, in fact, a progressive move recognising the historically and scientifically determined necessity of armed struggle.

However, in April 1976 Garba said, 'because we are getting disenchanted with the leadership of the ANC' requests from both Muzorewa and Nkomo for permission to visit Lagos had been turned down. Hence, in compliance with the OAU policy, the Federal military government decided to cut off direct aid to movements and factions in Zimbabwe and started channelling all assistance through the Liberation Committee and the government of Mozambique in the hope of bringing about a degree of leverage with which to promote unity. The Nigerian government indicated its position when presenting ₦133,400 ($250,000) to Mozambique for use in Zimbabwe. Garba explained, 'in normal conditions the cheque would have been sent to the unchallenged leader of Zimbabwe. Unfortunately, this person does not exist, the two liberation movements being busy fighting each other.'[7] At a later press conference, Garba called for a united front by saying,

Almost daily we hear that somebody has shot into prominence from virtually nowhere and the next day you hear that another person has gone down into obscurity. It is our hope that the nationalists [in Zimbabwe] will be able, even at this late hour, to forge a united front for the purpose of effective bargaining.[8]

The emphasis on national unity and the idea of effective bargaining are actually evasions of revolutionary positions. The Mohammed–Obasanjo regime, like the regimes of Nyerere and Kaunda stressed national unity as a core of their humanist policies of support, not to effect revolutionary change, but rather to encourage conditions for reconciliation and bargaining under efforts like the Anglo-American Proposals and the Lancaster House Talks.

Nevertheless recognition was, however, extended to the Namibian liberation movement, SWAPO. Sam Nujoma visited Nigeria in April 1976, and SWAPO was permitted to establish a permanent office in Lagos.

Ironically, there were fewer interactions between Nigeria and the liberation movements in South Africa though occasional delegations from South African movements visited Lagos. For example, the South African representative of the Pan-Africanist Congress was in Nigeria in September 1976 to hold talks with the Federal military government. He praised Nigeria's support for Angola as an encouragement to South Africa and referred to the 'popular uprising' in Soweto and elsewhere in South Africa as the beginning of the end for the apartheid government.[9] Despite this showering of praise, there was no direct support from the Federal government. The reason for this is not far to seek: owing to black South Africa's ethnic, regional and ideological variations and the consequent power struggles typical of African politics, there is a multiplicity of liberationist groups in South Africa. Hence, in January 1977 a joint communiqué was issued by Obasanjo and President Kaunda of Zambia in which Nigeria urged the two main groups, the PAC and ANC, to unite in a common front.[10]

Again, like its predecessors, the Federal military government of Mohammed–Obasanjo, in its 'war' against the segregationist and colonialist regimes of South Africa, Portugal and Rhodesia, adopted a series of social, economic and diplomatic measures of isolation, ostracism and deprivation. But unlike earlier Nigerian administrations, which had concentrated entirely on secondary sanctions, towards the end of the Obasanjo regime primary or direct sanctions were almost 100 per cent, while secondary sanctions – sanctions against other international actors, both state and non-state – were also instituted against those who might have dealings with the racist regimes. However, these latter sanctions were difficult to implement and took many forms. In August 1976, for instance, the passports of six members of the Nigerian Reformed Church wishing to attend an ecumenical meeting in Cape Town, South Africa, were seized by the Nigerian government. At the same time, Nigerian businessmen as well as foreign businessmen residing in the country were warned against having business connections with South Africans. Thus, there was a drastic curtailment of local trade; and to combat leakages the Federal government embarked upon a 'war' against retailers of contraband. In February 1977, the same month General Obasanjo so warmly received Andrew Young, visiting the country in his capacity as US ambassador to the United Nations, the Nigerian police, 'after a raid in search of South African goods . . . sealed the premises of a UTC store branch at Apapa and took away raisins apparently produced in South Africa'.[11]

Likewise, the Federal government under Obasanjo continued the policy of diplomatic isolation of the racist and imperialist regimes of Southern Africa. Indeed, beginning in the 1960s South Africa and Portugal were either driven out of international organisations or, where this failed, were subjected to harassment by walk-outs, votes of censure, non-recognition of credentials, or other radical international parliamentary techniques. With the rehabilitation of Portugal since 1975, the campaign has continued against South Africa. In September 1976, Nigeria was reported to be mounting a campaign to have South Africa barred from the International Atomic Energy Agency.[12]

Both at home and abroad, propaganda was mounted against racist enclaves in Southern Africa. Towards this end, the South African Relief Fund (SARF) was established in an effort to encourage public donations. Not only did the Head of State and his Deputy personally contribute ₦1000 ($1870) and ₦500 ($935) respectively, but in addition all civil servants in Nigeria gave up 2 per cent of their monthly income to the Fund.[13] The establishment of the Fund was hoped to stimulate similar action by 'sister' African countries.[14] It was during this period that the Voice of Nigeria, the external service of the Federal Radio Corporation of Nigeria, began broadcasting to South Africa in order to encourage freedom fighters in the battle against their colonialist overlords.

Given this background, and the relatively pleasant collaboration between Nigerian officials and Andrew Young, it would be a great oversight not to examine Nigerian–US relation during Young's period as US ambassador to the United Nations. The cordial relationship between the two countries from 1977 to 1983 might stimulate one's curiosity, given the fact that so many US corporations have vested interests in South Africa and that Nigeria, proclaimed the 'giant of Africa' by the West, played a major role in the anti-apartheid movement towards the end of the Ford–Kissinger years. US ties with South Africa did not drastically change when Young served as the US point man in Southern Africa, although the United States did support some sanctions under the so-called Sullivan Principles which had a limited effect in the country.[15]

While operating as the custodian of America's moderate neocolonial policy on the crisis in Southern Africa, Young discovered kindred spirits among Nigeria's military rulers and compradors. As he did everywhere he went on the African continent, Young appealed to the big-business interests of the Nigerian lumpen-bourgeoisie with a philosophy of pragmatism and interdependency. It appears that big-business interests were Young's greatest concern in Africa, and particularly in Nigeria, where the Southern Africa crisis seemed to play second fiddle (as most Nigerian intellectuals saw it) during the Carter and Obasanjo years.

During his September 1979 mission to Africa, Young indicated to the Nigerian–American Chamber of Commerce that the United States was buying about $5000 million worth of Nigerian oil per year. And, although he cleverly pointed out that Nigerians only solicited $1000 million of US business services,[16] he did not speak of how Nigerian crude oil is funnelled into other industries, which make big profits from the sale of petroleum and oil by-products in America's domestic and international markets: this would lead to a discussion of the perpetual technological imbalance which pervades the power relationship between developed and 'underdeveloped' nations. In addition, Young did not speak about the mounting oil glut or dollar–naira exchange rate, which at times stands at almost 2 : 1. As mentioned earlier, this mission to Nigeria was laced with several contracts, one of which (the Pullman–Kellogg) amounted to $500 million (₦333 million).

While these high-powered business deals were being made in the 'giant of Africa', the United States and her ally Britain persisted in strengthening their ties with South Africa. According to *Africa Contemporary Record*, South Africa's 'exports to the US shot up 70% in the first half of 1978 to $944.7 [million]', as compared to $553.9 million in the same period of 1977.[17] In 1979 when Andrew Young maintained (on the UN floor) the liberal position that South Africa has the right to participate in UN debates despite its apartheid policies and despite the attitude of underdeveloped countries which

wanted South Africa barred from the United Nations, 260 US corporations had investments in South Africa valued at R1565 thousand
million constituting 1 per cent of US foreign investment and over 15
per cent of all foreign investments in South Africa. Thus, in 1979 and
1980 allegations accusing the CIA and the US State Department of
shipping arms to South Africa through the Space Research Corporation, US–Canadian munitions company,[18] in breach of the UN embargo, badly soured US–African relations.

This was followed by another revelation. A Carnegie-sponsored
public opinion poll of 1000 American interviewees indicated, along
with the liberal sentiments of the respondents, the bulk of whom
condemned apartheid in South Africa, that '77% opposed US support
for organizations in [South Africa] which were willing to use violence'.[19]

British investments in South Africa were valued at £4000 million,
about 10 per cent of Britain's direct overseas investments, with a
portfolio investment estimated at £3000 million in 1979. Using United
Kingdom–South Africa Trade Association figures for 1979, *Africa
Contemporary Record* reported that Britain's gross total income from
trade with South Africa stood at £2000 million. It also reported that,
after a decline in British trade with South Africa in 1978, the new
Thatcher government had moved to make oil purchases easier for the
South African government and had also sent several trade missions to
the country during 1979, with the intention of sending still more in
1980.[20]

Even though the United States and Britain have never forgone
their ties with South Africa, their relations with its racist government
have experienced moments of tension. However, Africanists have
not taken such tensions seriously.

The material contradictions between, on the one hand, Nigerian
relations with the United States and its allies, particularly Britain,
and, on the other, the United States' Southern Africa policy are
indeed worthy of notice. A history and analysis of Nigeria's Southern
Africa policy and its commitment to Western powers may reveal
what made it and Andrew Young principal retailers of the Anglo-
American Proposals for Zimbabwe, and the moderate line on the
Southern Africa crisis.

The holding in Lagos from 22 to 26 August 1977 of the World
Conference for Action against Apartheid, in co-operation with the
OAU and the United Nations, was one of the greatest achievements
of Obasanjo's era. The Conference's aim was to maintain a complete
psychological isolation of South Africa and to expose the various

atrocities of the apartheid regime. With 112 governments, 112 inter-governmental organisations and a number of prominent individuals participating, the Conference was the largest international gathering ever held over the issue of apartheid.[21] In his opening speech, General Obasanjo reiterated Nigeria's moral and material support for the liberation movements in Southern Africa. He said, 'as long as the system of apartheid remains in Pretoria, aspirations for economic development and our fair share of the world's resources will be unattainable'.[22] Hence, an Economic Intelligence Unit was being established with the aim of barring foreign contractors who were known to have links with South Africa from tendering for any contracts in Nigeria.[23] Thus, the regime was embarking upon the effective application of pressure on countries that had relations with South Africa, principally the United States and Britain.

Indeed, Nigeria impressed upon the United States that it was not interested in improved bilateral relations so long as the United States continued its support for the status quo in Southern Africa. And in a speech at the United Nations, External Affairs Commissioner Garba indicated that

> The attitude of Nigeria to those countries that continue to support South Africa in the maintenance of its illegal presence in Namibia will continue to be re-examined and our relations with them will become increasingly dependent on their actions concerning the problem not only in Namibia, but in Southern Africa as a whole.[24]

In 1976 there were allegations of CIA involvement in the February coup attempt in which the head of state, Murtala Mohammed, was assassinated. In spite of this and the mounting tension between Nigeria and the United States over the Angola issue, the United States *remained an important customer for Nigeria's oil.*

Some Nigerians also suspected Britain of being involved in the attempted coup. In addition, the British government refused to extradite former Nigerian head of state Yakubu Gowon, who was living in Britain at the time and was under investigation by the Nigerian government for any part he might have played in the plot.

Another situation which caused tension in Nigerian–British rela-tions was the refusal by the British to lend the Nigerian government a sixteenth-century Benin ivory mask which it had chosen as the official symbol for the Festival of Arts and Culture (FESTAC). Neverthe-less, during this period Nigeria, as Britain's ninth-ranking trading-partner purchased £357.1 million of British goods, while South Africa, which ranked tenth, purchased some £346.8 million worth.[25]

Nigeria took part in the Commission set up by the 1977 Conference to consider proposals for further action against apartheid, with special reference to the promotion of increased political and material support for the oppressed people of South Africa and their national liberation movements, and to the implementation of the UN resolutions on apartheid. One of the resolutions of the Conference was to declare 1978 International Anti-Apartheid Year. This was observed in Nigeria with lectures, symposia and debates in the mass media and in various institutions of higher education. On one occasion Dr A. B. Akinyemi, Director of the Nigerian Institute of International Affairs, Lagos, delivered a lecture entitled 'Re-ordering Nigerian Foreign Policy' at the Club de Capital of the University of Ibadan.

There is no doubt, however, that Nigeria has been unsuccessful in seeking to apply pressure on countries doing business with South Africa. The Economic Intelligence Unit established in 1977 to monitor the activities of transnational corporations operating both in Nigeria and in South Africa has proved largely ineffective. In spite of its action against Barclays Bank International, which has branches in South Africa, the Unit has done little, lacking the sophisticated and efficient data-collecting system it requires to do its job properly. In fact, evidence shows that, in its urge for technology, Nigeria has been unable to carry out its threats against clients of South Africa. For instance, the US monthly *Business Magazine* reported during December 1977 that

> One purchase contract presented by the Nigerians contained a clause whereby Collins (a division of Rockwell International) would pledge not to do business with South Africa. The Collins negotiators hurdled with their lawyers and concluded that the United States law prevented their signing such a statement. So the Nigerians took back the contract and re-submitted it – minus the South African exclusion clause.[26]

The fact is that the decision to establish the Unit was impractical in view of Nigeria's level of economic and technological underdevelopment and dependence, and consequent inability to do without the services of firms that do business with South Africa. Policy-makers failed to recognise this, and thus proved unequal to the challenge the Unit presented. Another case in point is the fertiliser contract awarded to the Pullman-Kellogg Corporation of the United States by the Oba-sanjo regime in 1979, at the tail end of its existence. Also, judging from the vulnerable state of the Economic Community of West African States (ECOWAS), such a body as the Economic Intelligence Unit was from the outset bound to be a failure. This is because an embargo against South Africa's imperialist allies requires such a high level of economic co-operation with other West African countries that it would be impossible for any company opting out of Nigeria to transfer its services to any of the neighbouring countries with which Nigeria has free trade exchange. Such co-operation is at present notable by its absence.

Lastly, when we consider the fact that all the Western industrialised nations, including Japan, on which the developing countries are dependent for effective and durable transfer of technology have close trade links with South Africa, the decision to establish the Economic Intelligence Unit, laudable as it was, emerges as little more than a pious hope.

To have mounted an effective economic war against those enterprises doing business with South Africa, the Obasanjo regime would have needed to ensure

(1) a higher level of the economic growth in Nigeria than in South Africa (which is far from the case);
(2) the timely completion of the iron and steel complex in Warri and Ajaokuta;
(3) a high level of security and political stability in order to attract foreign investors other than those having connections with South Africa; and
(4) a higher return rate on investment than is available from South Africa.

South Africa's economy has been suffering over the past few years from internal political disorder, typified by the Soweto uprising and constant attacks by the guerrilla movement. Indeed, since the Soweto episode, foreign investors have been looking for other places to invest – especially in black Africa. The recent policy of the Ayatollah regime in Iran, calling for an oil embargo against South Africa, has also worsened the South African economy. The conversion of coal into oil as a way of overcoming the problem is extremely costly. If the worsening of the South African economy continues, Nigeria's use of economic weaponry against South Africa through primary and secondary sanctions is likely to become increasingly successful.

Be this as it may, in international gatherings and on any other suitable occasion, Nigeria's propaganda war against apartheid continued, with repeated statements by the Nigerian leadership of its commitment to wipe colonial evils from the African continent. In his statement on the anniversary of the International Day for the Elimination Of Racial Discrimination, Brigadier Garba said,

> In commemorating this day, the International Day for the Elimination of Racial Discrimination, we in Nigeria re-affirm our belief in the equality of all human beings irrespective of their race, creed or colour. We will do everything in our power to oppose and we will work strenuously for the total eradication of racial discrimination and apartheid.[27]

At the Libreville OAU Meeting in 1977, Nigeria charged other members to provide financial, moral and military backing to the liberation movements, as well as to the frontline states, because of its belief that the freedom fighters 'are not only fighting their cause, but our cause also, and . . . in their freedom lies our own dignity and security'.[28] Thus, Nigeria became the largest contributor to the OAU Liberation Fund, giving a yearly sum of about $5 million in bilateral aid to the freedom fighters in Southern Africa. In the first half of 1977, the Federal military government of Nigeria also provided the liberation movements with small amounts of arms and ammunition, as well as the services of two of its C130 Hercules military transport planes, and one of its 707 Boeing civilian aircraft,[29] Furthermore, in order to speed up the surrender of the white redoubts, the Nigerian Army Chief of Staff, retired General T. Y. Danjuma, made it known in June 1977 that the Federal government was prepared to send troops to assist the freedom fighters.[30] Barely three months later, General Obasanjo himself was reported to have said that, if Vorster's South African National Party government used nuclear weapons to defend the apartheid system, Nigeria was ready for it,[31] although what he had mind is far from clear.

However, things took a different shape towards the end of 1977. Relations between Nigeria and the United States, which had hitherto been at loggerheads, especially over the Southern Africa issue, became relaxed. So strong did the ties between the two governments become that their heads of state exchanged official visits – the first such in the history of US–Nigerian relations. As a result of the improvement, Nigeria, which in 1976 had rejected the Anglo-American Proposals for the settlement of the Rhodesian crisis, came out 'to give them a chance'. General Obasanjo even visited the frontline states to convince those countries to embrace the proposals.[32]

At that time Nigerian observers and students were asking themselves what had brought about this change in relations between the two nations. People began to wonder why the Nigerian leadership had thus befriended the US government. Dr Bala Usman was of the opinion that Obasanjo's visit to Washington was unnecessary, because the Carter Administration had not done enough to deserve a softening in Nigeria's attitudes.[33] Others felt that this sort of quick and sudden rapprochement with the United States would cause Nigeria to lose its credibility with more radical African states and with the freedom fighters.

In April 1978, during President Carter's visit to Nigeria (six months after Obasanjo had visited the United States), the two heads of state released a joint communiqué expressing their hope of a peaceful settlement in the Horn of Africa, and supporting the Anglo-American plan for Rhodesia, UN Security Council Resolution 385 for Namibian independence, Resolutions 242 and 338 on the Middle East crisis, and UN Charter principles – particularly those concerning Human Rights. During 1978 US exports to Nigeria were expected to exceed those to South Africa. In 1977 Nigeria was the United States' largest supplier of oil after Saudi Arabia, supplying oil to the value of $6200.1 million.[34]

There were many reasons for Nigeria's change of attitude. The internal and external environments dictated that it should pipe down in the pursuit of its erstwhile dynamic policy on Southern Africa. Indeed, coupled with President Carter's and Andrew Young's desire to see 'Human Rights extended to all races in Southern Africa',[35] during the second half of 1977 there was a pragmatic and opportunistic reappraisal of Nigeria's role in the area. Prior to this period, the Nigerian leadership was of the view that only through armed struggle could Southern Africa be liberated. Hence, as already pointed out, apart from financial aid, Nigeria provided direct military support to the liberation movements, though the offer of combat forces was received badly by other OAU states and rejected by the freedom fighters themselves.

Nevertheless, the official Nigerian government team sent to Zambia and Mozambique in July and August 1977 to evaluate the progress of the war against the white-minority regimes was disappointed by the slow advance of the campaign; and it reported that the freedom fighters could not hope to capture Salisbury for the next five years.[36] This marked the beginning of Nigeria's more moderate stand on the liberation question; and therefore the voice of the Nigerian leadership and the voice of Andrew Young had a similar pitch.

The 'abrasive style' of Nigerian ECOWAS diplomacy, stemming from the Mohammed–Obasanjo regime's insistence that the ECO-WAS headquarters should be located in Lagos, revived the distrust of the member states of the Communauté Economique des Etats de l'Afrique de l'Ouest for the larger ECOWAS. A further factor was Nigeria's refusal, in October 1977, to accept the OAU's designation of Niger as its candidate for one of Africa's two seats in the UN Security Council. Though Nigeria was eventually elected after several ballots, this nevertheless created considerable resentment in francophone West Africa. Nigeria's argument for deserving to represent Africa, at the Security Council was based on the fact that the following year (1978) was generally considered to be a crucial year for the liberation of Zimbabwe and Namibia, and since Nigeria had been called upon to contribute its forces to the UN peace-keeping force, it was logical that it should have a seat in the Council, where most of the important decisions concerning the liberation of Southern Africa were to be made.

But this rationale behind the government's stand did not escape criticism. At home, the criticism levelled against the government for jeopardising African unity stemmed partly from an article by Dr Bala Usman in which he expressed the view that Nigerian representatives would not be able to maintain an independent stance against the authority of the nominated British Resident Commissioner for Zimbabwe, Lord Carver.[37] Thus, the Obasanjo–Young alliance strongly implied that Nigeria would kowtow to the US position.

The fact that the period in question also witnessed a worsening of Nigeria's economic performance made the option of aligning with the United States almost inevitable.

In its budget of 1977, and in contrast to its initial commitment to do without foreign loans in its development, Nigeria started relying on foreign capital to execute its Third National Development Plan, 1975–80. This was owing to

(1) the continuing weakness of the American dollar in the world market, leading to losses of revenue to the Nigerian government amounting to ₦87 million ($156.6 million) in 1977, and forcing Nigeria's foreign reserves to fall from ₦3.7 billion ($6.666 billion) in December 1975 to ₦2.3 billion ($4.14 billion in February 1978;[38]

(2) a drop in the production of crude oil from 2.3 million barrels daily to about 1.9 million barrels, coupled with the fall in crude-oil prices; and

(3) the Federal Government's sudden budgetary decision to raise the original amount of public expenditure for the remaining plan period from ₦30 billion ($54.0 billion) to ₦42 billion ($75.60 billion).[39]

The net effect of all these economic difficulties was a recession in the country's economy. Hence, late in 1977 the Nigerian government borrowed ₦1.68 billion ($3.02 billion) from abroad – ₦534 million ($961.20 million) from the World Bank and the same again from West European banks.[40] Early in January 1978, the Federal government also signed a loan agreement for ₦534 million ($961.20 million) with some American and West European banks.[41] Overall, what this US–Nigerian rapprochement did was one-sided. It only bridged the gap of communication and understanding between an opportunistic Nigeria and the United States and her allies, and thus led to a renewal of confidence and sympathy between their reactionary leaderships.[42] The benefits of this 'good leadership' failed to rub off on the liberation movements.

Ostensible concessions were made by the West as a show of sympathy with black African states on the African liberation question. There was a repeal of the Byrd Amendment, which enabled US firms to import Rhodesian chrome; and the Nigerian leadership was consulted on the problem areas of Africa by both the United States and Britain, working hand in hand. The Western powers even laid down a code of conduct for the operation of their firms in South Africa and Namibia. However, neither these concessions nor the Nigerian propaganda campaign in favour of 'moderate change' produced any real change in Southern Africa. Indeed, in 1977 the US government voted against the UN Security Council sanctions on South Africa. All the US–Nigerian diplomatic efforts did was raise the expectations of the black people in Southern Africa while making the supremacist white regimes more recalcitrant.

The fundamental structure of the apartheid system did not change in the late seventies. Instead, a new Bantustan (so-called 'independent homeland'), named Bophutatswana, was created late in 1977. The new South African constitutional proposals providing for a powerful white executive president and three separate parliaments, one each for whites, coloureds and Indians, was a gimmick, and on its implementation in 1984 few coloureds and Indians bothered to vote.

The peaceful demonstrations of black school children in Soweto were brutally repressed by the apartheid regime in South Africa in June 1976. Also, the National Party government has outlawed eighteen black-consciousness organisations and pressure groups; and Steve Biko was murdered in cold blood in October 1977.

The South African regime still holds onto Namibia. The South African leadership wants to retain Walvis Bay, and does not want SWAPO to participate in Namibian elections. South African Prime Minister Vorster declared in January 1978 that, whether the New York independence talks on Namibia were successful or not, he would go on with elections and an internal settlement with only the Namibian internal political parties taking part; pending the outcome of these manoeuvres, he would grant Namibians independence that year.[43]

Instead of succumbing to the pressures of the liberation movements, Vorster's regime intensified its military campaigns against neighbouring states – Mozambique, Angola, Botswana and Zambia – which offered bases to the 'guerrillas' (African freedom fighters). In one of these exercises in Mozambique, in December 1977, about 1200 were reported to have died and many more wounded.[44]

In Rhodesia the story was the same. Smith rejected the Anglo-American Proposals because of

(1) their inclusion of the one-man, one-vote principle;
(2) the proposal to transfer control of the country's armed forces from whites to the proposed black government;
(3) fear of the Patriotic Front, especially since the Front's troops would form the basis of the future armed forces of an independent Zimbabwe.

It was therefore not surprising that the US–Nigerian accord over the Southern Africa issue proved ephemeral. Professor Aluko, a Nigerian university professor predicted a sudden collapse in US–Nigerian relations. He said that 'the "entente" would die a premature death and be given an unceremonious burial', especially with the election of a Republican President in the United States, and 'it would be "normal" rather than "special" relations between Nigeria and the United States'.[45]

Nevertheless, Nigeria did not give up the propaganda struggle against the obnoxious apartheid system. The Federal government under Obasanjo reverted to direct support of the liberation movements, although short of direct military involvement. It was this, among other things, that paved the way for the Lancaster House independence talks on Zimbabwe, and the final handing over of the reins of government to blacks in April 1980. It was to the same end that the Nigerian government nationalised the Nigerian assets of the buoyant Anglo-Dutch petroleum company Shell–BP, a move that for a short time had an adverse effect on the British economy.

5 Southern Africa and the Reagan Administration

The new posture in Washington since Reagan came to power in January 1981 has reversed the few achievements of the Carter Administration. The Reagan Administration's pro-South African posture has been clearly evidenced in leaked secret Department of State documents.[1] The new policy is embodied in the term 'constructive engagement', coined by Chester Crocker, Reagan's Assistant Secretary of State for African Affairs.[2] The aim of this policy is to get African support for US policy in Africa, especially in Southern Africa, as in the case of the recent US–Mozambique *rapprochement*.

This chapter examines and analyses US policy on Southern Africa since Zimbabwe independence, with particular attention to the Reagan Administration's policy since 20 January 1981.

During his election campaign for the presidency in 1980, Ronald Reagan said, 'the African problem is a Russian weapon aimed at us [the United States]'.[3] This statement could be interpreted to mean that the Southern Africa problem has turned into a confrontation between East and West. As far as Southern African affairs are concerned, Reagan is a novice. This was shown during his presidential campaign. He has very little knowledge of Africa and has made very few public statements on Southern Africa. His lack of knowledge about Africa and his simplistic views on Southern Africa have placed a cold-war confrontation in Southern Africa squarely on the East–West chessboard. Carter's regionalist approach to Southern Africa issues has been dismissed in favour of a cold-war stance – a process that, ironically, began under the Carter Administration itself, after the resignation of Andrew Young as US ambassador to the United Nations, and of Cyrus Vance as Secretary of State.

Late in January 1982, when Reagan was announcing his sanctions against Poland and the Soviet Union, the US Department of State and Department of Commerce were in the process of relaxing the US economic pressures against South Africa on the ground that such measures would not work. Reagan's announcement of economic sanctions against Warsaw and Moscow and his war of words (such as his propaganda message of 31 January 1982, 'let Poland be Poland' broadcast to the world through the Voice of America, and Radio Free Europe) were effectively diplomatic strategies to divert international attention away from the problems in Southern Africa especially the Namibian independence issue.

The Reagan Administration's pressure on Poland was meant to obtain the release to political prisoners, to end martial law and to reopen dialogue between the free trade union Solidarity and the Polish government. We must ask Reagan and his advisers why similar pressure could not have been exerted on the white-minority regime in South Africa, to eliminate apartheid, and obtain the release of thousands of blacks, and give the 22 million disenfranchised blacks a political voice in the running of the South African government.

After Reagan entered the White House, he took a more sympathetic attitude towards South Africa. and the South African government took the best advantage of this. To Prime Minister P. W. Botha and his white racist clique, President Reagan's conciliatory policy was an excuse to put off such questions as Namibian independence and the so-called 'internal reform'. The South African government looked upon the US foreign policy agenda as being already full of more urgent issues, such as the Polish crisis, arms control, the deployment of strategic nuclear missiles in Europe, the Afghanistan problem, the Middle East and El Salvador conflicts, and the disarray of the NATO alliance. Consequently the Reagan Administration was, and still is, dragging its feet on Southern Africa, particularly the Namibian independence issue.

Chester Crocker advised the Administration to come to some minimal level of agreement about the question of South Africa, and to steer a course between the twin dangers of abetting violence in the Republic of South Africa and aligning itself with the cause of white rule. According to Jeane Kirkpatrick, Reagan's ambassador to the United Nations, 'racial dictatorship is not as bad as Marxist dictatorship'.[4] It is no wonder, then, that the US government should support racist, authoritarian, repressive and corrupt regimes around the world, such as the Duvalier regime of Haiti, the military juntas in Chile and Argentina, the late Shah of Iran (1953–79), Portugal imperialists until the 1974 revolution, as well as reactionary groups in El Salvador and UNITA in Angola. Reagan himself has said on several occasions that the United States will not abandon South

Africa, because of its strategic importance to the West in the production of essential minerals.

Both the Rockefeller Commission Report published in May 1981[5]
(this Commission was formed during the Carter Administration) and
Reagan's adviser on African affairs agreed that South Africa is very
important and should not be neglected by the West. The motives
behind Reagan's co-operation with Pretoria involve, as with all other
US administrations, keeping the Cape sea route open for the transportation of Western oil, ensuring exports of essential minerals from
South Africa, and promoting just enough concessions to Human
Rights to avert racial violence within South Africa. Given all this, US
policy-makers hope, American investment interests both in South
Africa and elsewhere on the continent will be secured and Soviet
influence in Africa curbed. The US policy towards Southern Africa in
the 1980s is just a continuation of the Nixon–Kissinger policy of the
1970s,[6] because the basic thrust of both the Reagan policy and the
Rockefeller Commission Report is that the United States must remain a constructive influence in South Africa. Both, again, reject
economic sanctions and disinvestment measures against South Africa, because, so the argument runs, black people in South Africa
would suffer most, and Western Europe, especially Britain is unwill-
ing to go along with any economic sanctions against Pretoria.[7] The
argument that black people in South Africa would suffer most from
economic sanctions is baseless. We do not completely deny that a
withdrawal of Western transnationals from South Africa would hurt
many blacks economically, but this would be a short-term sacrifice to
achieve a meaningful and lasting political solution. In any case, since
blacks have been suffering since the arrival of the white man at the
Cape in 1652, suffering is not new to them and the new generation of
South African blacks is prepared to go through any hardship to
achieve genuine freedom.

Since 1979, South Africa's white regime has been waging an
undeclared war in Southern Africa in collaboration with the Mozambique National Resistance (MNR) in Mozambique, the Savimbi-led
rebel group, UNITA, and the newly formed Military Committee for
Angolan Resistance (COMIRA) in Angola. Also, South Africa has
been promoting the assassination of ANC leaders living in Botswana,
Mozambique and Zimbabwe. The aims of South Africa in carrying out
all these clandestine activities are, first, to destabilise the whole of the
Southern Africa sub-continent; second, to delay Namibian independence; and third, to undermine the efforts of the Southern African

Development Coordination Conference (SADCC).[8] The latter is a new regional economic co-operation aimed at liberating, economically, the nine independent black-ruled states of the region from Pretoria.

What is most interesting is that the resistance in Mozambique is led by the Shona ethnic group from central Mozambique, which is the same nationality to which Mugabe, Prime Minister of Zimbabwe, belongs. It would seem that given the ideological and revolutionary ties between Machel and Mugabe, the Zimbabwean Prime Minister would have intervened in the conflict between the MNR and FRELIMO much sooner than he did, so as to unify the forces in Mozambique. It was not until the summer of 1985 that Mugabe, who came to power in 1980, committed 10,000 troops and other forms of military aid to FRELIMO.

Nevertheless, US–South African relations have not suffered as a result of South Africa's clandestine activities. Thus, the USA is as much involved in the destabilisation of the region as its South African ally.

South Africa is part of the Western capitalist system; hence, the exigencies of US domestic politics virtually rule out disengagement. The US government has no political will to bring about pressure on Pretoria. The circumstances encourage Prime Minister Botha to go no further than cosmetic internal reforms. South Africa has refused to sign the Nuclear Nonproliferation Treaty and yet the Reagan Administration supplies enriched uranium to South Africa for use in its nuclear programme. Namibian independence is threatened because Reagan continues to link the Namibian solution to the withdrawal of Cuban troops from Angola. South Africa, sensing positive encouragement from the White House, has hardened its illegal hold on Namibia, while its 'hot pursuit' raids into Angola and Mozambique have become almost a daily affair.[9] President Reagan sees South Africa as a strategically valuable ally of the West. Thus, US relations with South Africa are a priority item in the Reagan Administration's policy towards Southern Africa.

Since Reagan entered the White House, the relationship between black Africa and the United States has reached a crucial turning-point. Cultural and educational exchange programmes with Africa are either being sharply reduced or cut off completely by the Administration, and Africa is suffering more in this respect than the rest of the Third World. Above all, the Reagan Administration's African policy is accommodating the apartheid regime in Pretoria. South Africa has now become a close Western ally. The Reagan Administration has started to claim that the problems in Southern Africa, and especially Namibia, are not errors of apartheid policy or the white-minority rule in South Africa, but rather the result of the Cuban and Russian presence in Angola, and Soviet assistance to SWAPO in Namibia and the ANC in South Africa. As already stated, the Administration now views South Africa as a Western outpost and not as a Western outcast. Logically, the Administration's new cold-war stance draws South Africa and the Western nations, led by the United States, into close military co-operation with each other. The apartheid regime in South Africa is looked up to by the United States as a strong ally in its fight against Soviet and Cuban influence in Southern Africa. President Reagan's Republican predecessor, Gerald Ford, had after all used the same argument to encourage and fund a CIA paramilitary operation in Angola between 1975 and 1976.[10]

The Reagan Administration recently relaxed regulations that prohibit the export of non-military goods to the South African armed forces and police, contending that the move would convince Prime Minister Botha that South Africa is better off pursuing a so-called reformist course. In the past, Botha has been willing to risk international disfavour in the interests of Afrikaner unity. Our belief is that he will do so again.

The Reagan Administration has assumed that the Soviet and Cuban presence in Southern Africa can be removed in the context of a Namibian settlement, and that the UNITA rebel group led by Jonas Savimbi is an important factor in the Angolan situation. In actual fact, there is no prospect of military victory for UNITA in Angola, despite the financial and military assistance afforded it by the US government. In May and September 1981, the Reagan White House sought to link a Namibian settlement with the withdrawal of Cuban troops in Angola and insisted it needed its hands free of the restraining bonds of the Clark Amendment, which forbade US aid to South African-backed UNITA.[11] The aim was to destabilise the MPLA government in Angola, and to push the dubious US linkage of a Namibian settlement to Cuban withdrawal from Angola. President Reagan's former Secretary of State, General Haig, argued, 'there is an empirical relationship between the ultimate independence of Namibia and the continuing Soviet and Cuban presence in Angola'.[12]

A great controversy surrounded the Clark Amendment. The Reagan Administration argued that the Amendment improperly tied the President's hands in formulating and conducting foreign policy. It blames the measure for the failure of the Ford and Carter administrations to dislodge the Soviets and Cubans from Angola. Although, at first, the Reagan Administration failed to get Congress to repeal the

Amendment, it flirted with the idea of extending recognition to Jonas Savimbi's UNITA in order to force a political showdown in Angola by creating a military stalemate. In January 1982 in Rabat, Morocco, Savimbi said 'material help is not dependent on nor limited by the Clark Amendment. A great country like the United States has other channels.'[13] These and like comments tend to lend credibility to allegations of US subversion made by Angola News Agency, which in March 1982 reported that COMIRA had been formed in close collaboration between the Reagan Administration and Savimbi's UNITA as a replacement for the defunct FNLA and was training 2000 men in northern Angola.

According to Chester Crocker, US interests in Africa are 'supporting regional security . . . ensuring the US and [their] allies' petroleum and non-fuel minerals . . . promoting trade and investment . . . cooperating with . . . Western allies and friends in Africa to deter aggression and subversion by adversaries'.[14] It is clear that South Africa is the main country to which Crocker refers. The Reagan Administration has already vowed to oppose any move to impose mandatory comprehensive sanctions against South Africa. This was demonstrated in May 1981, when the United States joined France and Britain to veto a UN Security Council resolution seeking to impose mandatory economic sanctions against South Africa. The decision of the United States to allow five South African military officials to visit the country in May 1981 was another signal that it did not have the political will to bring pressure on Pretoria. The South Africans had discussions with US State Department officials, and even with the US ambassador to the United Nations, Jeane Kirkpatrick, in her office in the UN building in New York.[15] When South Africa invaded Angola on 23 August 1981, international condemnation was swift. West Germany and Britain summoned South Africa's ambassadors in their respective countries to urge immediate withdrawal of South African forces from Angola. The only Western country that refused to condemn South Africa was the United States.

The leaked Crocker memorandum concerning meetings with South African leaders in Pretoria on 15–16 April 1981 confirmed previous indications that the Reagan Administration was willing to open a new phase of bilateral ties between Washington and Pretoria. Referring to South Africa as a part of the Western system, it was in this document that Crocker said that the exigencies of US domestic politics 'virtually rule out disengagement'.[16] Thus, Crocker recommended a deceitful policy of steering 'between the twin dangers of abetting violence in the Republic of South Africa and aligning the United States with the courses of white rule.'[17] This is in line with US policies which support the apartheid regime of South Africa.

With the Ambassador Kirkpatrick saying, 'racial dictatorship is not as bad as Marxist dictatorship',[18] with Crocker, Reagan's chief adviser on African affairs, advocating a US alignment with the South African minority regime, and with Reagan's support coming from American big business and conservative quarters, we should expect thorough and continuing US support for the racist regime in South Africa.

I THE UNITED STATES AND THE NAMIBIAN INDEPENDENCE ISSUE

The United States received much of the copper mined in Namibia (Southwest Africa) during the German colonial period, and ultimately accounted for 7 per cent of all exports from the territory, second only to Germany's 82 per cent.[19] Furthermore, the United States played a key role in Germany's economic exploitation of Namibia by providing German colonial secretaries access to American research facilities relating to agricultural commodities which could be produced in Africa.[20] Many Americans assisted in the exploration of the territory by directly managing commercial operations there. Most notable of these Americans was Gardner Williams of Saginaw, Michigan, who was an associate of Cecil Rhodes and who later became the first general manager of De Beers Consolidated Mines.[21] In 1982 there were 130 American corporations operating in Namibia (some of which are listed in Table 1), and over 200 in South Africa (a partial list appears in Table 2).

Without doubt, it is difficult for a state voluntarily to initiate or support an action the result of which would jeopardise its own interests. It is precisely the United States' economic interests that have made it so reluctant to take concrete action against South Africa to ensure Namibia's independence.

II THE CONTACT GROUP, THE UNITED NATIONS AND THE NAMIBIAN ISSUE

Between 1977 and 1980, the Carter Administration brought about a few changes in American foreign policy on Namibia. It organised a concerted action on the part of the 'Western Five', now known as the

TABLE 1 *Some of the US companies operating in Namibia by 1982*

Company	Date of arrival
General Motors	1920s
Ford Motors	1920s
Farrell Lines	1925s
Chrysler	1930s
Caltex	1937
Tsumeb Corporation	1947
American Motors	1947
Pan American	1947[a]
Goodyear	1947
Johnson and Johnson	1947[a]
Eastman Kodak	1947
Colgate-Palmolive	1950
Bethlehem Steel	1952
IBM	1952
Uniroyal	1953[a]
Star Kist Foods	1954
Parker Pens	1954[a]
General Electric	1956[a]
Quaker Oats	1956[a]
Coca Cola	1958
Chase Manhattan	1959[a]
Marine Diamond	1962[a]
Getty Oil	1963
Standard Oil of California	1963
Texaco	1963
Gulf Oil	1965
National Cash Register	n.a.
Minnesota Mining and Manufacturing	n.a.
Phillips Petroleum	1972[a] [b]
Mobil Oil	1976[c]
Holiday Inns	1976

[a] Estimated date.
[b] Ceased operating in Namibia in 1974 (all other companies still operating).
[c] Date of incorporation in Namibia.

SOURCE Allan D. Cooper, *US Economic Power and Political Influence in Namibia 1700–1982* (Boulder, Col.: Westview Press, 1982) pp. 129–31.

Contact Group, to share responsibilities for resolving the conflict over Namibian independence. The US deputy ambassador to the United Nations, Donald McHenry, and representatives from Britain, France, West Germany and Canada started shuttle diplomacy between the United States, Namibia and South Africa, meeting with SWAPO leader

TABLE 2 *Some of the US corporations operating in South Africa by 1982*

AAF International
Abbott Laboratories
Addressograph Multigraph
AFIA
American Cyanamid
American Express*
Arthur Anderson
Applied Power
Automated Building Components
Batten, Barton, Durstine and
   Osborn
Berkshire International
Black Clawson
Blue Bell
Borden
Borg Warner
Bristol Myers International
Bucyms Erie
Caltex Petroleum*
Carborundum
Cascade
J.I. Case
Caterpillar Tractors
Celanese
Chase Manhattan*
Cheeseborough-Ponds
Chrysler*
Citibank*
Coca Cola Export
Colgate-Palmolive
Columbia Broadcasting Systems
Columbus McKinnon
Control Data*
CPC International
Dames and Moore
Dart Industries
John Deere
Del Monte
DHJ Industries
Donaldson
Dow Chemicals
Dresser Industries
Dubois International
Dunn and Bradstreet
Eastman Kodak*
Echlin Manufacturing
Englehard Minerals and Chemicals

Envirotech
Esso Africa
J. A. Ewing and McDonald
F & M Systems
Ferro
Firestone Tire and Rubber*
Ford Motors*
Gardner-Denver
Gates Rubber
General Electric*
General Motors*
Gillette
Goodyear Tire and Rubber*
Heublein International
Honeywell International
International Business Machines
International Flavors and
   Fragrances
International Harvester
International Telegram and
   Telephone*
Johnson and Johnson
S.C. Johnson and Sons
Kellogg*
Kendall
Kidder Peabody
McGraw-Hill
Macmillan Publishing
M & T Chemicals
Manufacturers Hanover
Masonite
Max Factor
Measure
Merck, Sharp and Dohme
Geo. J. Meyer Manufacturing
Miles Laboratories
Minnesota Mining and
   Manufacturing
Mobil Oil*
Monsanto
Nabisco
Nashua
National Cash Register*
National Chemearch
National Standard
National Starch and Chemicals
Newmont Mining

TABLE 2 *Continued*

A. C. Nielson International	Riggs Bank
Norton	Robbins
Otis Elevator*	A.H. Robins
Pan American	Rockwell International*
Parker Pens	Helena Rubinstein
Parke, Davis	Schering Ploughs
Parker Hannifin	Scholl
Perkin–Elmer	G.D. Searle
Permatex	Singer
Pfizer International	Tampax
Phillips Bros	Timkin
Phillips Petroleum*	Titan
Pizza Inn	Trane
Precision Valve	Twentieth-Century Fox
Preformed Line Products	Union Carbide*
Ramsey Engineering	Uniroyal International
Revlon	United States Steel
Rexnord	Westinghouse Electrics
Richardson-Merrell	

* Major US multinationals operating in South Africa.

SOURCE   Adapted from *US Corporate Interests in South Africa*, Report to the Committee on Foreign Relations United States Senate, by the Senate Subcommittee on African Affairs (Washington, DC: Government Printing Office, 1978) pp. 85–94.

Sam Nujoma, and other Namibian nationalist leaders, the Nigerian[22] and frontline states' leaders, and representatives of the white regime in South Africa.[23]

The Contact Group had agreed to work with the United Nations to exert pressure on South Africa to grant independence to Namibia after a peaceful transition. The United States supported UN Security Council Resolution 435 of 1978, which required the UN Secretary-General to appoint a special representative for Namibia, 'in order to ensure early independence through free and fair elections under the supervision, and control of the United Nations Transition Assistance Group (UNTAG)', and to assist him in carrying out his mandate. It also supported the proposal for a settlement of the Namibian situation submitted by the Contact Group.[24]

All the efforts of the world body to get the Contact Group to persuade South Africa to accept the UN plan for Namibian indepen-

dence failed in 1978. The apartheid regime was increasingly antagon-
istic towards America's black negotiators for Namibian independence,
and relations between the US Administration and the Botha regime
in South Africa worsened in 1979 and 1980,[25] until Reagan entered
the White House in 1981.

III THE LINKAGE APPROACH OF THE REAGAN ADMINISTRATION

Reagan's Republican administration has jeopardised the negotiations
for Namibia's independence by gradually and diplomatically aban-
doning the UN plan and the Contact Group approach initiated by the
Carter Administration. It has changed its predecessor's Human
Rights approach to an anti-terrorism approach, labelling SWAPO a
terrorist organisation, and seeing a link between the independence
struggle in Namibia, strong Soviet support for SWAPO and the
Cuban military presence in neighbouring Angola. As a result, resolution of the Namibian problem is made to depend on removal of the
'communist threat in Angola, and Namibia's future is no longer the
simple issue it should be. The country has been turned into a
battleground for the preservation of South African and Western
economic and political interests.[26]

Since the victory of the liberation movement in Zimbabwe, the
apartheid regime in South Africa has shifted its policy on Namibia
and is entrenching itself in the territory, using it as a buffer zone in
defence of South Africa. The consequence of this is the complete
militarisation of Namibia. South African military personnel are not
confined to active service in the so-called operational area: they have
assumed control of most levels of the territory's administration.

This development has not been helped by the intervention of the
Reagan Administration since 1981. Its obsession with the communist
'threat' in the developing world means that it sees the presence of
Cuban troops in Angola as more important than the question of
Namibia's independence. This is the major stumbling-block to a
negotiated independence settlement for Namibia.

Southern Africa has again become an area of East–West competi-
tion in anticipation of what Reagan's former Secretary of State,
General Alexander Haig, called 'the era of resource war'. South
Africa is a US ally in the battle.

IV THE STRATEGIC IMPORTANCE OF NAMIBIA TO THE UNITED STATES

With the resurrection of the cold war and the increasing strain on US–Soviet relations, there has been an upsurge in the articulation of hardline neo-conservative thinking in Washington. Central to Reagan's policy on Namibia is the war cry of 'anti-communism'. This is why he would say, 'the African problem is a Russian weapon aimed at us [the United States]'.[27] South Africa, to the Reaganites, is helping to contain the Soviets while safeguarding Western strategic concerns in Southern Africa.

Strategically Namibia is important to the United States and the Western world as a whole. Namibia is the largest producer of gem diamonds in the world and a leading producer of chromium, manganese, platinum, uranium, vanadium and numerous other minerals. In most cases the only major producer of these strategic minerals outside Southern Africa is the Soviet Union especially for the production of chromium. Chromium, manganese and vanadium are indispensable in the production of steel. Platinum-group metals serve as catalytic agents in refining petroleum and in reducing automobile emissions. These four minerals imported from Namibia and South Africa, are essential to Western industry and defence.[28]

Uranium-mining has increased Namibia's strategic importance to the United States because of its use in producing nuclear weapons. This is one of the major reasons why Reagan has argued that the United States cannot abandon South Africa: it is 'strategically essential to the Western world in its production of minerals'.[29] An American company, Tsumeb Corporation, accounts for most of the base-metal mining in Namibia, and the Namibians provide the cheapest labour for such enterprises.[30]

V ZIMBABWE AND ITS AMERICAN CONNECTION

On 18 April 1980 the independent nation of Zimbabwe emerged from a seven-year war (1972–9) for national liberation. The Carter Administration rushed to embrace Prime Minister Mugabe's regime and offered it diplomatic relations and economic aid, despite Mugabe's Marxist leanings. At the independence celebrations, the Carter Administration promised to contribute $45 million between 1980 and 1982 for the reconstruction of war-torn Zimbabwe.[31]

The United States under Carter regarded Zimbabwe as a pivotal experiment in black–white peacemaking that could lead the way to a peaceful solution in Namibia, and even in Zimbabwe's white-ruled neighbour, South Africa. Andrew Young, who as US ambassador to the United Nations led the US delegation to the Zimbabwean independence celebrations, remarked, 'I would like to see South Africa learn the lesson of Zimbabwe.'[32]

Prime Minister Mugabe has adopted a moderate, non-aligned foreign policy which can be characterised as pragmatic. This approach has helped Zimbabwe to attract many international private and non-private investors.

Since the Reagan Administration entered the picture, US–Zimbabwe relations have remained cordial. The United States has been one of the largest donors of aid for development programmes in Zimbabwe. Mugabe's policy of welcoming foreign investment from the private sector into Zimbabwe has been well received in Washington.

Following independence, in March 1981, Zimbabwe received a $2000 million boost when some forty-five countries and a number of international financial institutions around the world pledged this amount for economic and social-development programmes at the Zimbabwe Conference on Reconstruction and Development (Zimcord) in Harare (formerly Salisbury). Zimcord has formed the basis of all aid programmes ever since. The aim of the Conference was to secure the financial underpinning needed to overcome the dislocations caused by the war, and to aid the government's long-range objectives of 'rapid economic growth, full employment, dynamic efficiency in resources allocation and an equitable distribution of the ensuing benefits'.[33]

At Zimcord the United States pledged $250 million, of which $50 million was for a commodity-import programme to enable the private sector to import raw materials, with the United States paying the foreign currency and the private sector paying the Zimbabwean government the equivalent in local currency.[34] The money generated from this by the government, which in effect is getting something for nothing, will be used for development programmes. These include agricultural training-centres, irrigation projects and housing-schemes. The Reagan Administration has also guaranteed $25 million for a high-density housing-scheme in Harare to provide 4000 houses.[35]

The severe setback that the Soviet Union encountered in Zimbabwe in the wake of Mugabe's election victory in 1980 has been a big gain for the United States diplomatically. It has done everything possible to take advantage of the Soviets' setback, which has come about because Moscow backed the Nkomo-led ZAPU instead of the rival Mugabe-led ZANU before the formation of the Patriotic Front. Thus, the USSR maintained rather distant relations with Mugabe even after the Front came into being, and found itself at least temporarily shut out of Zimbabwe at the time of its independence. 'It was not until 1981 that Mugabe's government agreed to open formal diplomatic relations with Moscow.'[36]

It is obvious that Mugabe's approach to relations with the present US Republican administration is much like that of China, which supported ZANU during the period of armed struggle. As relations between China and the USSR became more strained, China's relations with the United States improved. While Sino-Soviet relations were not ideal before Chairman Mao's death, Peking was none the less defiant of US imperialism. In recent years the Chinese leadership has, in view of its tradition of international relations, been unusually cordial towards the United States. What is ironic is that the current leaders of both China and Zimbabwe, which have been so impressive in revolutionary history, are now seen as potential friends by Western conservative administrations. At a time when the United States boldly engages in gunboat and big-stick diplomacy in the Caribbean (Grenada), Central America (Nicaragua and El Salvador) and the Middle East (Lebanon), China and Zimbabwe appear as impotent pragmatists in the scheme of international politics.

Because of its sponsorship of a series of progressive UN resolutions,[37] Zimbabwe is mending some of its contradictions. But, in terms of Sino-Soviet relations, its foreign policy must begin to be one of positive support for improvement, rather than one of mere partisanship.

6 Conclusion

The historic appointment of Andrew Young as US ambassador to the United Nations was predicated on a history of political collaboration between, on the one hand, willing petty-bourgeois black American integrationists and African and other Third World nationalists, and, on the other, monopoly capitalists and imperialists of the developed nations. Suffice it to say that the economic success of the latter is closely interrelated with the economic backwardness of the former (poorer) groups and nations.

The pragmatic concerns of the world's leaders and the interdependence of national economies have led political systems in contradictory directions. Hence, in the underdeveloped world, 'even a system based on social justice and a democratic constitution may need backing up by emergency measures of a totalitarian kind'.[1]

The political state in underdeveloped nations has emerged from the intersection of external and internal pressures of the international capitalist economy and of class conflicts at both the national and international levels.

Without doubt, Andrew Young understands the history, politics and economic consequences of international relations with regard to the underdevelopment and dependence of the Third World nations. Yet, like American Southerners who ignored the atrocities perpetrated by the Ku Klux Klan, the former UN ambassador avoided a radical critique of the present state of the world economy and the class conflicts in underdeveloped nations. This was evidence of his client role in the consolidation of worldwide capitalist interests.

The racialism that gave visibility to the Civil Rights movement in America was Young's calling-card in the underdeveloped world. By virtue of his Civil Rights background he was accepted as a champion of peoples of colour everywhere. Young's opposition to racial inequality indeed qualified him for playing a role in the Southern Africa crisis, but his official ties to the US government and his moderate outlook prevented him from making a positive contribution to the solution of that crisis.

103

The concept of 'inequality', so popular in Civil Rights literature, is not in itself enough to explain the Southern Africa crisis today, any more than it suffices to explain the Civil Rights movement or the African independence movement of the past three decades. Important as Young's commitment to racial equality and Human Rights have been in ensuring his reputation, it is inconceivable that the limitations of these concepts were not apparent to him or to the international actors with whom he aligned himself. In spite of race, creed or colour, inequalities will always exist under capitalism. However, the concept loses significance under true socialism.

The problem facing the political economy of Southern Africa, like that facing world capitalism as a whole, is structural.[2] Hence, the mere replacement of white regimes with black regimes does not alter, in any positive way, a political economy which, particularly in the case of capitalist and peripheral capitalist nations, includes some and excludes others. What it boils down to is the relationship between superstructure and base – that is, between the cluster of administrative, judicial, legislative and ideological institutions, on the one hand, and capital, on the other. It is the structure of these variables and the interaction between them that needs changing. However, to change one is, owing to their interrelationship, to change all, and this needs to be borne in mind in instituting any structural change.

But what, then, is the real purpose of structural change in Southern Africa? What, in other words, are the revolutions of Mozambique, Angola and Zimbabwe (and those that will follow them) all about? And why did they culminate in armed warfare?

This structural change or revolution represents a transformation of the structural determinants of surplus appropriation (the distribution of excess cultural and material wealth) at the local, national and international levels. The tensions which permeate this process of change are rooted in the dialectical interaction of class interests and in the conflicts of group interests within classes. Class tension (for example, between labourers and owners) is broad and often pronounced, while internal group tensions (for instance, between commercial/agricultural capitalists and industrial/financial capitalists), may be less obvious to the layman but are sometimes more devastating.

Historically, in Southern Africa, as in the whole of Africa, there are three major divisions of interests, between external capitalists (transnational corporations); indigenous compradors and state bureaucrats (this group represents a cluster of interests); and labourers.

Certainly this is oversimplified; the divisiveness is more dynamic and relationships are constantly changing. Limiting an analysis of class interests in Africa to these three sectors will not explain the tension between agricultural capitalists and peasants in African societies, and certainly this relationship needs changing too.

As quiet as they may keep about it, Western governments have very little respect for the governments of underdeveloped nations, because they realise the disastrous potential of internal conflicts in these countries for Western investors who have money and property tied up there. As a means of keeping a handle on what we have come to know as 'instability', and as a means of protecting profits in their underdeveloped client states, Western powers create and rely upon authoritarian and autocratic regimes, such as the former Samoza regime in Nicaragua, and may be prepared to use interventionist tactics, as in the case of CIA operations in Chile in 1973.

From the vantage point of the monopoly capitalists, these are viable options for containing and controlling the internal conflicts in African and other Third World countries. Nevertheless, the violent coercion of puppet regimes who protect Western interests has grave consequences, as can be seen from the Stanleyville massacre in the Congo (Zaire) in 1964, and the Bakolori massacre in Sokoto, Nigeria, in 1980. It is such coercion of the peripheral capitalist state that begets armed warfare in the same way as hunger begets crime. The realities of this oppression and its wretched and bloody manifestations say something about the complex problems that faced Andrew Young when serving under President Carter.

Young is like so many petty-bourgeois types or their imitators who join the dominant structure and perpetuate the status quo, rationalising the values and tactics of the system with 'trickle-down' theories and the fear of communist aggression. (The latter is not necessarily a phobia of Young). Looking back on all we have said, the point must be made that our critique and analysis of Young and all the international actors (the United States, Britain, Nigeria, South Africa, Israel, and so on) involved in the Southern Africa question are not based upon a conspiracy theory. In addition we realise that the history of nations and their relationship to the capitalist world economy (or to the phases of development and underdevelopment) makes equal economic productivity by different states inconceivable, although even in this context more socially responsive and democratically determined political economies could diminish problematic relations. Rather, we are calling attention to the events of a worldwide struggle in which individuals, groups, classes and nations take actions that inevitably heighten internal and external tensions in political economies.

Appendixes

APPENDIX 1   LETTERS TO ANDREW YOUNG

NOTE   All letters addressed to the Honorable Andrew Young, Mayor of Atlanta, Mayor's Office, City Hall, Atlanta, Georgia 30335, and signed Dr H. E. Newsum.

8 June 1982

Dear Mr Young,

For almost three years I have been putting together a book tentatively entitled 'Andrew Young and Beyond: American Foreign Policy Towards Southern Africa'. [sic] This manuscript grew out of a forty-two page seminar paper which I presented in the Department of Political Science at the University of Ife in Nigeria in May 1980. That seminar paper was entitled 'The Andrew Young Affair Revisited', which is now Section 2 of the present manuscript [Ch. 1].

Later, at the beginning of 1981, Dr. Layi Abegunrin was invited to co-author the text with me. Dr Abegunrin is a lecturer in the Department of International Relations at the University of Ife; he contributed three sections of the manuscript. The titles of Dr Abegunrin's sections are: Section 3 – 'The Central Intelligence Agency (CIA): Covert Operations in Southern Africa, with Special Reference to Angola' [Ch. 2]; Section 4 – 'The Carter Administration's Policy on Southern Africa, 1977–1980' [Ch. 3]; and Section 5 – 'Nigeria, South Africa and the United States Connection: Myth and the Western-Proclaimed 'Giant of Africa' [Ch. 4]. [Abegunrin later also contributed Ch. 5.]

Section 5 will be followed by a conclusion which I have yet to compose.

I have the good fortune of getting Professor Harold Cruse of the History Department at the University of Michigan [sic] to write the Introduction to the book. The Introduction will comprise Section 1 of

the manuscript and is tentatively entitled 'Pan-Africanism and the
Black Petty-bourgeoisie'. [The idea of an Introduction was later
dropped.]

The ideological thrust of the manuscript is neo-Marxist. We first
discuss your political thinking which we believe to be reflective of
Civil Rights strategies. We borrow three concepts from two contemporary black political scientists. From Matthew Holden's *The Politics
of the Black 'Nation'* we have borrowed the concepts of 'clientage'
and 'opposition', and from Manning Marable's, 'Tuskegee, Alabama: The Politics of Illusion in the New South', *Black Scholar*, May
1977, we have borrowed the concept of 'deference' politics (a concept
which Marable borrowed from *Black Power* by Carmichael and
Hamilton). Thus, our approach to analysing your political thinking is
historical. In the present work we look at the strategies, tactics and
social consciousness which evolved from the Civil Rights movement
in which you played an active part as a SCLC strategist. Recently I
have attempted an in-depth quantitative or statistical analysis of your
1975 Congressional voting-record in an effort toward further illumin-
ating your political thinking. If possible you might help me in the
latter effort by informing me about where this kind of quantitative
analysis of your Congressional voting-record has already been done.

Our historical understanding of Civil Rights politics in the United
States coupled with our understanding of political and economic
developments in American foreign policy on Southern Africa in
particular, and on Africa and the Third World as a whole, form the
basis of our critique of you when serving as the United States
Ambassador to the United Nations. Our information sources are too
many to list in this letter; however, some of your speeches in African
countries have become our primary sources.

It is hoped that you would agree to a telephone interview with me.
I would appreciate it if, when replying to this letter, you would give a
date and time I can call you in your office for this purpose. I have only
five questions I would like to ask as follows:

1. Is there a firm agreement between the Nigerian Government and
   Pullman-Kellogg on the 1979 fertiliser contract, or was the deal
   abandoned?
2. Did you represent Pullman-Kellogg in the negotiation of the
   fertiliser contract with the Nigerian Government?
3. Are you close to or friendly with General Obasanjo, M. O. K.
   Abiola, and Yur Adua in Nigeria?

4. What was the purpose of your visit with Polisario guerrillas in early 1980?
5. Is your brother Walter as involved in economic relations with Africa as you are?

I am presently working on the section of the book in which these questions are of primary importance and I would be most grateful if you would answer them as soon as possible so as not to delay the completion of the book.

We have tried as best as possible to be objective in our analysis and critique of you. You must, however, bear in mind that our ideological perspective runs counter to the political, economic and intelligence approaches of United States foreign policy on Africa. I am looking forward to a very pleasant interview with you in the near future. I have enclosed a copy of my Curriculum Vitæ for your information.

11 June 1982

Dear Mr Young,.

Further to my June 8, 1982 letter regarding my manuscript, 'Andrew Young and Beyond: American Foreign Policy Towards Southern Africa', I am enclosing the *Professional Biography* of Dr Layi Abegunrin who is co-authoring the book with me.

Again I am looking forward to a pleasant interview with you.

17 August 1982

Dear Mr Young,
The completion of my manuscript ('Andrew Young and Beyond: American Foreign Policy Towards Southern Africa') is pending a telephone interview with you. I would be most grateful if you would indicate a time and date I can call you in your office during this month of August.

7 September 1982

Dear Mr Young,

On several occasions I have phoned your office for the purpose of obtaining a telephone interview with you. I have corresponded with you in writing at least three times, but have not received a reply. As I have explained to your press secretary, Mr Ossenberger, and as I have explained in my letters to you, I am in the process of producing a manuscript dealing with American foreign policy towards Southern Africa and the specific role you played in this arena of international affairs while serving as the United States Ambassador to the United Nations.

Having failed to get an interview with you, I have decided not to further prolong the submission of the manuscript to prospective publishers. The interview would have aided me in avoiding speculations about your participation in US–African affairs. As it is, I must make some speculations and I only hope that these will not cause either you or me embarrassment.

I assure you that my co-author and I have tried to be fair to you in our analysis and critique of you as a principal actor in US–African relations.

APPENDIX 2   ANDREW YOUNG'S 1975 CONGRESSIONAL VOTING-RECORD, RELATIVE TO THAT OF RON DELLUMS* AND RALPH METCALFE[†]

		Progressive[a]	*No vote*[b]	*Counter-Progressive*[c]	*Total*
Military					
Dellums	(no.)	43	0	10	53
	(%)	81.13	0	18.87	100
Metcalfe	(no.)	37	3	13	53
	(%)	69.81	5.66	24.53	100
Young	(no.)	38	0	15	53
	(%)	71.70	0	28.3	100
Bureaucratic					
Dellums	(no.)	47	0	16	63
	(%)	74.6	0	25.4	100
Metcalfe	(no.)	36	14	13	63
	(%)	57.14	22.22	20.63	100
Young	(no.)	39	2	22	63
	(%)	61.9	3.17	34.92	100
Energy					
Dellums	(no.)	61	0	13	74
	(%)	82.43	0	17.57	100
Metcalfe	(no.)	40	18	16	74
	(%)	54.05	24.32	21.62	100
Young	(no.)	48	1	25	74
	(%)	64.86	1.35	33.76	100
Commercial					
Dellums	(no.)	117	0	16	133
	(%)	87.97	0	12.03	100
Metcalfe	(no.)	90	24	19	133
	(%)	67.67	18.09	14.29	100
Young	(no.)	98	13	32	133
	(%)	73.68	2.26	24.06	100

APPENDIX 2 *Continued*

		Progressive[a]	*No vote*[b]	*Counter-Progressive*[c]	*Total*
Social					
Dellums	(no.)	219	1	16	236
	(%)	92.80	0.42	6.78	100
Metcalfe	(no.)	181	34	21	236
	(%)	76.69	14.41	8.90	100
Young	(no.)	205	1	30	236
	(%)	86.86	0.42	12.71	100
Total					
Dellums	(no.)	487	1	71	559
	(%)	87.12	0.18	12.70	100
Metcalfe	(no.)	384	93	82	559
	(%)	68.69	16.64	14.67	100
Young	(no.)	428	7	114	559
	(%)	76.56	1.25	22.18	100

NOTE   For details on the specific issues voted on see *Congressional Quarterly Almanac, 94th Congress, 1st Session 1975*, vol. XXXI (Washington, DC: Congressional Quarterly, 1976).

[a] A vote is considered 'progressive' if it mainly benefits the population at large or those groups which are powerless in American society.
[b] A 'no vote' means the Congressman has either voted 'present' without expressing an opinion or the *Congressional Quarterly* could not find out his opinion. (The 'votes' in this table cover all ways in which a Congressman can let his opinion concerning a bill or resolution be known.)
[c] A 'counter-progressive vote' is one which benefits mainly large business corporations and their owners, top level military personnel and others who are in positions of power. A 'no vote' on these bills is considered progressive.
* Ron Dellums, congressman from California, has enjoyed a reputation for being a champion for peace, social welfare, civil rights, and environmental protection. He is perceived by his California constituency and other observers as a progressive spokesman in the US Congress.
† Ralph Metcalfe, congressman from Chicago, Illinois, maintained consistent popularity among his constituency and throughout the US; however, his voting record in Congress was troubled by his relative conservatism and failing health.

SOURCE   Gerald A. Bennett, 'An Analysis of Conservative, Liberal and Progressive Members of the Black Caucus' (research in progress).

APPENDIX 3   RHODESIA: PROPOSALS FOR A SETTLEMENT

Presented to Parliament by the Secretary of State for Foreign and Commonwealth Affairs by Command of Her Majesty, September 1977

FOREWORD

The British Government, with the full agreement of the United States Government and after consulting all the parties concerned, have drawn up certain proposals for the restoration of legality in Rhodesia and the settlement of the Rhodesian problem. These proposals are based on the following elements:

1   The surrender of power by the illegal regime and a return to legality.
2   An orderly and peaceful transition to independence in the course of 1978.
3   Free and impartial elections on the basis of universal adult suffrage.
4   The establishment by the British Government of a transitional administration, with the task of conducting the elections for an independent government.
5   A United Nations presence, including a United Nations force, during the transition period.
6   An Independence Constitution providing for a democratically elected government, the abolition of discrimination, the protection of individual human rights and the independence of the judiciary.
7   A Development Fund to revive the economy of the country which the United Kingdom and the United States view as predicated upon the implementation of the settlement as a whole.

A full account of the proposals is attached. The first of the Annexes to the proposals outlines the principal points of the proposed Independence Constitution; the second Annex deals with the Constitutional arrangements during the transition period; and the third Annex relates to the Development Fund. The precise provisions of the Independence Constitution will have to be elaborated in further detailed discussions with the parties and in due course will be

considered at a Constitutional Conference to be held during the
transition period.

It is impossible at this stage to lay down an exact timetable: but it is
the intention of the British Government that elections should be
held, and that Rhodesia should become independent as Zimbabwe,
not later than six months after the return to legality. To achieve this it
will be necessary to proceed as quickly as possible after the return to
legality to the registration of voters, the delimitation of constituencies, the detailed drafting of the Constitution and its enactment under
the authority of the British Parliament.

PROPOSALS FOR A SETTLEMENT IN RHODESIA

1   On 10 March 1977 the British and United States Governments
    agreed to work together on a joint peace initiative to achieve a
    negotiated settlement in Rhodesia. The objective was an indepen-
    dent Zimbabwe with majority rule in 1978.

2   To succeed, any settlement must command the support of those
    people of goodwill of all races and creeds who intend to live
    together in peace as citizens of Zimbabwe. Amongst these
    people there are now many conflicting interests and views. There
    is an atmosphere of deep distrust. The armed struggle has led to
    the loss of many lives and to much human suffering. The econ-
    omy has been gravely weakened. But there is surely one over-
    riding common interest, that peace should be restored and that
    government with the consent and in the interest of all the people
    should be established.

3   In April the British Foreign and Commonwealth Secretary,
    Dr Owen, toured the area and met all the parties to the problem as
    well as the Presidents of the five Front-Line States, the Prime
    Minister of South Africa and the Commissioner for External
    Affairs of Nigeria. He set out the elements which, taken together,
    could in the view of the two Governments comprise a negotiated
    settlement, as follows:

    (*a*) A Constitution for an independent Zimbabwe which would
        provide for –

        (1) a democratically-elected government, with the widest poss-
            ible franchise;

(2) a Bill of Rights to protect individual human rights on the basis of the Universal Declaration of Human Rights. The Bill would be 'entrenched' so that amendment of it would be made subject to special legislative procedures and it would give the right to an individual who believed his rights were being infringed to seek redress through the courts;

(3) an independent judiciary.

(*b*) A transition period covering the surrender of power by the present regime, the installation of a neutral caretaker administration whose primary role, in addition to administering the country, would be the organisation and conduct of elections in conditions of peace and security and the preparation of the country for the transition to independence. This period, it was envisaged, would be as short as possible, and in any case not more than six months.

(*c*) The establishment of an internationally constituted and managed development fund (the Zimbabwe Development Fund).

4 Following that tour, Dr Owen and the United States Secretary of State, Mr Vance, met in London on 6 May and agreed to carry forward their consultations with the parties on the basis of these proposals. To this end they established a joint consultative group. The group met all the parties on a number of occasions in London and in Africa and carried out detailed technical discussions with them. In parallel, the Governments of interested countries have been kept informed generally of the progress of the consultations.

5 On the basis of these consultations the British Government, in full agreement with the United States Government, have now decided to put firm proposals forward, covering the three aspects of the problem described in paragraph 3 above. In doing so they emphasise that the three aspects are intimately linked and must be judged as a whole. It is impossible for every single aspect of a settlement to be acceptable to everyone. The best, if not the only, hope for a settlement is a balanced and fair package in which, though no one may achieve all their aims, everyone can see hope for the future.

The Constitution

6 It is proposed that the Independence Constitution should provide that Zimbabwe would be a sovereign republic. Provision would be made for democratic elections on the basis of one man, one vote and one woman, one vote, for a single-chamber National Assembly. Elections would be on the basis of single member constituencies. Detailed constitutional proposals are set out at Annex A. The proposals should not necessarily be taken as excluding alternative possibilities in certain areas which do not go to the heart of the Constitution: e.g. provision is made for an executive President with a Vice-President, but there might instead be a constitutional President and a Prime Minister, in which case many of the powers which it is proposed to vest in the President would be vested in the Prime Minister or would be exercised by the President on the advice of the Prime Minister.

7 Discrimination would be forbidden by a Bill of Rights protecting the rights of individuals. As described above (para. 3 (*a*) (2)), this Bill of Rights would be entrenched in the Constitution and would be justiciable so that aggrieved individuals could enforce their rights through the courts. The Bill of Rights would permit the Government of Zimbabwe to introduce measures of land reform while guaranteeing the right to private property. The Constitution would also establish an independent judiciary and an independent Public Service Commission to ensure an efficient and non-political civil service.

8 The Government of Zimbabwe would inherit the assets and debts of the Government of Southern Rhodesia and would take over past and present pensions obligations in the public sector, the rights of the pensioners being guaranteed by the Constitution. The Constitution would contain the basic provisions regulating Zimbabwe citizenship and these would be entrenched. The question whether there should be any restrictions on the possession of dual citizenship and, if so, whether there should be an extended period during which the choice would have to be made would be a matter for further discussion with the parties.* (*Any citizen of the United Kingdom and Colonies who surrenders his citizenship in order to retain or acquire the citizenship of another member of the Commonwealth is entitled to regain United Kingdom citizenship subsequently under the British Nationality Act 1964.)

9 The Commonwealth Governments in London expressed the unanimous hope that Zimbabwe would soon become a member of the Commonwealth. The British Government will do everything to facilitate this.

The Transition

10 It is a basic premise of the British and United States Governments that the present illegal regime will surrender power so that the transitional administration may be installed peacefully. The two Governments will take such steps as seem to them appropriate to secure the transfer of power by Mr Smith (or his successor) on a day to be agreed.

11 The British Government will place before the Security Council their proposal for the Independence Constitution (Annex A) and also their proposal for the administration of the territory of Rhodesia during the transition period leading up to independence. The latter will comprise the following elements:

(*a*) The appointment by the British Government, either under existing statutory powers or under new powers enacted for the purpose, of a Resident Commissioner and a Deputy. The role of the Resident Commissioner will be to administer the country, to organise and conduct the general election which, within a period not exceeding six months, will lead to independence for Zimbabwe, and to take command, as Commander-in-Chief, of all armed forces in Rhodesia, apart from the United Nations Zimbabwe Force (see below).

(*b*) The appointment by the Secretary General of the United Nations, on the authority of the Security Council, of a Special Representative whose role will be to work with the Resident Commissioner and to observe that the administration of the country and the organisation and conduct of the elections are fair and impartial.

(*c*) The establishment by resolution of the Security Council of a United Nations Zimbabwe Force whose role may include:

(1) the supervision of the cease-fire (see below);
(2) support for the civil power;
(3) liaison with the existing Rhodesian armed forces and with the forces of the Liberation Armies.

The Secretary-General will be invited to appoint a representative to enter into discussions, before the transition period, with the British Resident Commissioner designate and with all the parties with a view to establishing in detail the respective roles of all the forces in Rhodesia.

(d) The primary responsibility for the maintenance of law and order during the transition period will lie with the police forces. They will be under the command of a Commissioner of Police who will be appointed by and responsible to the Resident Commissioner. The Special Representative of the Secretary-General of the United Nations may appoint liaison officers to the police forces.

(e) The formation as soon as possible after the establishment of the transitional administration, of a new Zimbabwe National Army which will in due course replace all existing armed forces in Rhodesia and will be the army of the future independent State of Zimbabwe.

(f) The establishment by the Resident Commissioner of an electoral and boundary commission, with the role of carrying out the registration of voters, the delimitation of constituencies and the holding of a general election for the purposes of the Independence Constitution.

On the agreed day on which power is transferred to the transitional administration (para. 10 above), a cease-fire will come into effect within Rhodesia and measures will be taken to lift sanctions.

12   An outline of the Transitional Constitution is at Annex B.

The Zimbabwe Development Fund

13   The Zimbabwe Development Fund, jointly sponsored by the British and United States Governments, will have as a target a minimum approaching US$1000 million and a maximum rather less than US$1500 million to which Governments in many parts of the world will be asked to contribute. Its purpose will be to provide funds for the economic stability and development of an independent Zimbabwe through assistance to various sectors and programmes such as rural development, education, health, social and economic infrastructure, and resettlement and training schemes for Africans, including those affected by the present conflict. The operations of the Fund would help to ensure that the obligations of

the Zimbabwe Government under the settlement will not inhibit economic development in Zimbabwe for lack of foreign exchange and would thereby also help to reassure those who might fear that the new Government might be unable to carry out these obligations. The establishment and continued operation of the Fund are predicated upon the acceptance and implementation of the terms of the settlement as a whole. A more detailed account of the proposed Fund is at Annex C.

Conclusion

14   The British and the United States Governments believe that the above proposals provide for all the citizens of the independent Zimbabwe security, but not privilege, under the rule of law, equal political rights without discrimination, and the right to be governed by a government of their own choice. They also believe that the proposed arrangements for the transfer of power are calculated to ensure a quick, orderly and peaceful transition to independence. They have agreed to use their joint influence to the full to put the proposals into effect. But a lasting settlement cannot be imposed from outside: it is the people of Zimbabwe who must achieve their own independence. These proposals offer them a way. The two Governments urge them to seize the opportunity.

ANNEX A   INDEPENDENCE CONSTITUTION

Status of Zimbabwe

1   On independence Southern Rhodesia will become legally known as Zimbabwe. The Constitution will provide that Zimbabwe will be a sovereign Republic with the Constitution as its supreme law.

The Head of State

2   (*a*) There will be a President of the Republic. Candidates for President will have to be citizens of Zimbabwe and will be subject to the same qualifications and disqualifications as candidates for election to the National Assembly.

   (*b*) Elections to the office of President will take place at the same time as general elections to the National Assembly and the Constitution will provide that the successful presidential candidate will be the one who has been endorsed by at least half of the successful candidates for election as Elected Members of the National Assembly.

(c) A President will usually hold office until a new President is elected (or he himself is re-elected) at the next general election to the National Assembly. However, there will be provision for his removal from office for physical or mental incapacity or because of his violation of the Constitution or other gross misconduct. Such removal will take place if (but only if) a recommendation to that effect is made by a judicial tribunal appointed on the initiative of the National Assembly: the Constitution will prescribe the procedure to be followed.

(d) When the President's office has become vacant in the above way or because of death or resignation, the Vice-President (see paragraph 3 (b) below) will succeed to the office. The Vice-President will also discharge the functions of the office of President during the latter's absence from the country or during any temporary incapacity.

(e) The President's emoluments, which will be determined by Parliament, will be charged on the Consolidated Fund and may not be reduced during his tenure of office. The Constitution will also provide for the President's personal staff.

(f) The President will be immune from suit or legal process during his tenure of office.

The Executive

3 (a) The executive powers of the Republic will be vested in the President who will discharge them, subject to the Constitution, either directly or through officers subordinate to him.

(b) The President will appoint a Cabinet consisting of a Vice-President and a limited number of other Ministers, from among the Members of the National Assembly. The President will himself preside over the Cabinet. The Vice-President and other Ministers will hold their offices at the President's pleasure.

(c) Each department of government will be in the charge of a Minister and the President may himself take charge of one or more departments and the Cabinet will be collectively responsible to the National Assembly of the government of the Republic.

(*d*) The Vice-President will be the Government leader in the National Assembly but the President himself will have the right to participate in its proceedings though not to vote.

(*e*) The President may also appoint a limited number of junior Ministers from among the Members of the National Assembly.

(*f*) The Constitution will establish the offices of the Secretary to the Cabinet and Permanent Secretaries of departments. All these will be civil service officers but there will be special provisions (see paragraph 7 (*e*) (v) below) regulating the appointment and tenure of the holders.

(*g*) The office of Attorney-General, who will be the principal legal adviser of the Government of the Republic, will be held by a Minister.

(*h*) There will be a separate office of Director of Public Prosecutions which will be an office in the civil service. The Director of Public Prosecutions will have final control over the initiation, conduct and discontinuance of prosecutions and, in the exercise of that power, will not be subject to direction or control by any other person or authority. However, the Attorney-General will be entitled to bring to his attention any considerations of public interest which may be relevant to any particular case. The appointment, tenure and terms of office of the Director of Public Prosecutions will be specially provided for (see paragraph 7 (*e*) (vi) below).

(*i*) The Prerogative of Mercy will be vested in the President. There will be an Advisory Committee on Prerogative of Mercy which the President will be obliged to consult in all capital cases and which he will be able to consult in any other case. But he will not be bound to act in accordance with its advice.

(*j*) The President will be the Supreme Commander of the armed forces of Zimbabwe.

Parliament

4 (*a*) The Parliament of Zimbabwe will consist of the President and a single-Chamber National Assembly.

(*b*) The National Assembly will consist of [100]* Elected Members (but see sub-paragraph (*f*) below).* The precise number of seats remains to be decided in negotiation with the parties.

(*c*) The Elected Members will be returned, in elections con-
ducted on the 'simple majority' principle, by single-Member
constituencies containing as nearly as possible equal numbers
of registered voters.

(*d*) The delimitation of constituencies will be carried out at
prescribed intervals by an independent Electoral Commission which will also supervise the registration of voters and
the conduct of elections.

(*e*) The franchise for the election of the Elected Members will be
based on universal adult suffrage, i.e. all Zimbabwe citizens
of the age of 21 and upwards who have been registered as
voters and who are not specifically disqualified (e.g. on
grounds of insanity, criminal conviction, etc.).

(*f*) The Constitution will also provide for [20]* Specially Elected
Members who will be elected by the Elected Members of the
Assembly after each general election. The purpose of providing for the Specially Elected Members will be to give
adequate representation to minority communites. The exact
way in which the Constitution should achieve this will be a
matter for further discussion. After an initial period (the life
of two Parliaments or eight years, whichever is the longer)
Parliament may abolish the seats of the Specially Elected
Members or alter the arrangements which are designed to
secure minority representation. Such a provision may be
made by a simple Act of Parliament requiring no special
majority and no special procedure and it will take effect at
the next succeeding dissolution of Parliament. But no such
change may be made during the initial period and the relevant provisions of the Constitution will, during that period, be
unamendable. *The precise number of Specially Elected
Members will be one-fifth the number of ordinary Elected
Members (see footnote, para. 4 (*b*) above).

(*g*) All Members of the National Assembly must be citizens of
Zimbabwe who are themselves qualified as voters and are
not subject to one of the specified disqualifications (e.g.
insanity, criminal conviction, holding public office, etc.).

(*h*) Subject always to the provisions of the Constitution, Parliament will have full power to make laws for Zimbabwe.

(*i*) Parliament's power to make laws will be exercised by bills passed by the National Assembly and assented to by the President.

(*j*) When a bill is presented to the President for his assent, he will be free, acting in his discretion, to give or withhold his assent. But if he withholds his assent, the bill will be returned to the National Assembly which may, within six months, present it once more for the President's assent. If a bill is so re-presented, the President must then either give his assent or dissolve Parliament.

(*k*) The President may summon, prorogue or dissolve Parliament at any time but there must be a session of Parliament at least once in every year and not more than six months may elapse between sessions. There must be a general election within two months of any dissolution. If Parliament has not been earlier dissolved by the President, it will stand dissolved automatically at the end of five years after a general election.

(*l*) If the National Assembly at any time passes a vote of no confidence in the Government, the President must either dissolve Parliament or resign his own office.

Fundamental rights

5   (*a*) The Constitution will contain provisions ('the Bill of Rights') on the lines of those in the Constitutions of other recently independent Commonwealth countries protecting fundamental human rights and freedoms. These will guarantee:

   (i) the right to life;
   (ii) the right to liberty of the person;
   (iii) protection from slavery and forced labour;
   (iv) protection from inhuman treatment;
   (v) protection from deprivation of property: this will confer protection from expropriation of property except on specified grounds of public interest and even then only on condition that there is prompt payment of adequate compensation (the amount of which, if not agreed, can be determined by an independent tribunal), and that the compensation may be remitted abroad within a reasonable period. It will be expressly provided that, where

undeveloped agricultural land is compulsorily acquired for the purpose of encouraging its development, the compensation payable to the former owner may disregard any value which might attach to the land by reason of its potential development and should take into account only the original purchase price and any other actual expenditure on it, e.g. the cost of physical improvements;

(vi) the right to privacy of home and other property;

(vii) the right to a fair trial in civil and criminal proceedings;

(viii) freedom of conscience;

(ix) freedom of expression;

(x) the right of individuals, groups or communities to establish and maintain schools at their own expense, provided that such schools are not operated on a discriminatory basis;

(xi) freedom of association (especially to form and operate trade unions);

(xii) freedom of movement (including the freedom to leave Zimbabwe and the immunity of Zimbabwe citizens from expulsion from Zimbabwe);

(xiii) freedom from discrimination.

(b) These fundamental rights will be justiciable, i.e. any person who asserts that they have been, are being or are likely to be infringed in his case will be able to apply to the High Court for that question to be determined and, when appropriate, for redress.

(c) It follows from the fact that the Constitution is to be the supreme law of Zimbabwe (see para. 1 above) that any law which conflicts with the Bill of Rights will to the extent of that conflict, be void and that any executive action that so conflicts will, to the same extent, be unlawful. This applies in particular to laws or practices that are discriminatory. Most of the discriminatory laws and practices now in operation will in fact have been terminated by the transitional administration before independence (see para. 9 (a) of Annex B) but there may be a few which are still in existence when the independent Government of Zimbabwe takes over. It will presumably be the intention of that Government to terminate them as soon as possible thereafter but in some cases it may still not be possible to do so at once since the first

Government of Zimbabwe may need a little further time in which to work out the new laws or new arrangements to take their place. To this limited extent, therefore, the Constitution will permit the Government of Zimbabwe to continue these existing laws and practices, notwithstanding the Bill of Rights, for such time as it takes to replace them but in any case for no longer than two years from the date of independence. No new discrimination will, of course, be lawful and the Constitution will expressly provide that, if any existing law or practice is amended or replaced during that period, no greater degree of discrimination may be introduced than was lawful before that amendment or replacement.

(*d*) The Constitution will permit certain of the provisions of the Bill of Rights to be derogated from during periods of public emergency. For this purpose, a public emergency will be deemed to exist when it has been proclaimed by the President but any such proclamation must either have received prior approval by a resolution supported by two-thirds of all the Members of the National Assembly or must be ratified by such a resolution within a week after it was made. The proclamation will lapse within a further three months unless the National Assembly's approval has in the meantime been renewed by a similar majority.

The Judicature

6 (*a*) The Constitution will establish a High Court, which will be divided into an Appellate Division and a General Division, and there will also be such subordinate courts as Parliament may from time to time provide for.

(*b*) The judges of the High Court will be a Chief Justice and such other judges (either Justices of Appeal or Puisne Judges) as Parliament may prescribe.

(*c*) The Chief Justice will be appointed by the President, acting in his discretion.

(*d*) The other judges of the High Court will be appointed by the President in accordance with the advice of the Judicial Service Commission (see sub-para. (*h*) below).

(*e*) The Chief Justice and other judges of the High Court will not be removable from office (until retiring age) except on grounds of physical or mental incapacity or misconduct, as

determined by a judicial tribunal in accordance with a procedure which the Constitution will prescribe.

(*f*) The terms of service of the judges of the High Court (including their emoluments, which will be charged on the Consolidated Fund) may not be altered to their disadvantage during
their tenure of office.

(*g*) The power to appoint, exercise disciplinary control over, and
remove from office the judges of the subordinate courts and
certain other officers connected with the High Court (e.g.
Registrar) will vest in the Judicial Service Commission.

(*h*) The Constitution will establish an independent Judicial Service Commission consisting of the Chief Justice, another
judge of the High Court designated by the Chief Justice, and
a member of the Public Service Commission (see paragraph 7
below) designated by the Chairman of that Commission.

The Public Service

7 (*a*) The Constitution will establish an independent Public Service Commission consisting of a Chairman and four other
members.

(*b*) The members of the Public Service Commission, who must
not be (or have recently been) public officers or Members of
the National Assembly or otherwise actively engaged in
politics, will be appointed by the President for a fixed term
and will not be removable during that term except for physical or mental incapacity or misconduct, as determined by a
judicial tribunal in accordance with a procedure to be prescribed by the Constitution.

(*c*) The terms of service of the members of the Commission
(including their emoluments, which will be charged on Consolidated Fund) may not be altered to their disadvantage
during their tenure of office.

(*d*) Subject to certain specified exceptions, the power to appoint
persons to hold or act in public offices, to exercise disciplinary control over persons so appointed and to remove them
from office will vest in the Public Service Commission. (The
term 'public offices' includes all civil-service offices and offices in the police force but not offices in the armed forces.)

(*e*) The specified exceptions are as follows:

(i) offices on the President's personal staff: these will be within the President's personal control, though he may arrange with the Public Service Commission for regular public officers to be seconded to his staff:

(ii) offices of the judges of the High Court and other offices within the jurisdiction of the Judicial Service Commission;

(iii) officers on the staff of the National Assembly: before exercising the relevant powers in the case of these officers, the Public Service Commission will need to obtain the concurrence of the Speaker of the Assembly;

(iv) offices in the police force: the relevant powers in the case of the Commissioner of Police himself will be vested in the President, acting after consultation with the Public Service Commission; in the case of other members of the police force they will be vested in the Commissioner of Police or in such officers subordinate to him as may be provided for by any law in that behalf or, subject to any such law, as he may delegate them to;

(v) the offices of Secretary to the Cabinet, Permanent Secretaries and Zimbabwe Ambassadors abroad: the relevant powers will be vested in the President, acting after consultation with the Public Service Commission;

(vi) the office of Director of Public Prosecutions: the power to appoint a person to this office will be vested in the President, acting after consultation with Public Service Commission and the Judicial Service Commission, but a Director of Public Prosecutions will not be removable from office (until retiring age) except for physical or mental incapacity or misconduct, as determined by a judicial tribunal in accordance with a procedure to be prescribed by the Constitution, and his terms of service (including his emoluments, which will be charged on the Consolidated Fund) may not be altered to his disadvantage during his tenure of office;

(vii) the office of Auditor-General: the power to appoint a person to this office will be vested in the President, acting after consultation with the Public Service Commission; once appointed, the Auditor-General will be protected in the same way as the Director of Public Prosecutions.

(*f*) The Constitution will protect the pensions of all public officers including past officers) by:

    (i) charging them on the Consolidated Fund;

   (ii) a provision which will ensure that the pensions of officers who are compulsorily retired to facilitate the reconstruction of the public service can be freely remitted abroad; and

  (iii) preventing the law regulating the payment of a public officer's pension from being altered to his disadvantage after the commencement of his service.

Finance

8   (*a*) The Constitution will establish a Consolidated Fund into which all public revenues (not otherwise payable by law into some other public fund) will be paid.

   (*b*) The Constitution will require annual estimates of expenditure to be laid by the Government before the National Assembly for its approval and will provide for the passage by Parliament of Appropriation Acts to authorise such expenditure. No monies will be allowed to be withdrawn from the Consolidated Fund or any other public fund except under the authority of such an appropriation or when they are charged by the Constitution or some other law on that fund.

   (*c*) The Constitution will provide for a Contingencies Fund and for other procedures for authorising unforeseen expenditure.

   (*d*) The Constitution will establish the office of Auditor-General whose duty it will be to monitor the above requirements, to audit the accounts of Government and other public authorities and to report on these matters direct to the National Assembly.

Citizenship

9   (*a*) The Constitution will establish Zimbabwe citizenship and will contain the basic provisions relating to it. Parliament will be authorised to make supplementary legislation regulating the acquisition and loss of Zimbabwe citizenship within the limits permitted by the Constitution.

   (*b*) All persons who are citizens of Southern Rhodesia (whether by birth, descent, adoption, naturalisation or registration) immediately before independence will become Zimbabwe citizens automatically on independence.

(*c*) All persons who have the right immediately before independence, to apply to become citizens of Southern Rhodesia will have a similar right, within a specified period after independence, to apply to become Zimbabwe citizens.

(*d*) All persons born in Zimbabwe after independence will be Zimbabwe citizens by birth.

(*e*) Any person born outside Zimbabwe after independence whose father is a citizen of Zimbabwe by virtue of his birth in Zimbabwe (or in Southern Rhodesia) will be a Zimbabwe citizen by descent.

(*f*) A woman who is married to a citizen of Zimbabwe after independence will have the right to become a citizen of Zimbabwe herself.

(*g*) Whether the Constitution should permit dual citizenship (with or without restrictions) is a matter for further discussion. If it is not permitted, a citizen of Zimbabwe who acquires the citizenship of another country by voluntary act (other than marriage) will automatically lose his Zimbabwe citizenship, while a citizen of Zimbabwe who involuntarily acquires the citizenship of another country (e.g. by birth) must either renounce that other citizenship (or, if that is not possible, make a prescribed declaration) within, say, five years of the relevant event (or of attaining the age of 21 years) or lose his citizenship of Zimbabwe. Similarly, a person who, at independence, automatically becomes a citizen of Zimbabwe and is also a citizen of another country will have to renounce his other citizenship (or make the prescribed declaration) within five years of independence, failing which he will lose his Zimbabwe citizenship, and a person applying for Zimbabwe citizenship will have to renounce his existing citizenship (or make the prescribed declaration).

(*h*) Parliament will be empowered to provide for additional grounds upon which persons may acquire Zimbabwe citizenship or lose that citizenship (but may not take away the citizenship of persons who have it by birth or descent or who have automatically acquired it at independence).

Amendment of Constitution

10 (*a*) All provisions of the Constitution will be amendable by Act of the Zimbabwe Parliament. But the Constitution will prescribe

the procedure to be followed for effecting such an amendment. These will vary according to the extent to which the provisions to be amended go to the basic structure of the Constitution or are especially sensitive.

(*b*) Some provisions, e.g. those prescribing the maximum number of Ministers, will be amendable by simple Act of Parliament: no special majority and no special procedure will be required.

(*c*) Most provisions will be amendable by an Act of Parliament which has been passed at its final reading in the National Assembly by a majority of two-thirds of all the Members of the Assembly. But a Bill for an Act to amend such a provision must also have been published in the Official Gazette at least thirty days before first reading and a period of at least three months must elapse between first reading and final reading.

(*d*) A limited number of provisions (e.g.) those dealing with citizenship, with fundamental rights and with the judicature and, of course, those prescribing the procedure for constitutional amendment) will be amendable only by a bill which has satisfied the requirements in (*c*) above in two successive sessions, in between which Parliament has been dissolved and a general election has taken place.

(*e*) In addition, there will be a very few provisions which will not be amendable at all for a specified limited period after independence. These will be the provisions dealing with fundamental rights, the provisions relating to the Specially Elected Members in the National Assembly and the provisions prescribing the procedure under (*d*) above. A bill to amend any of these provisions will not be capable of being introduced in the National Assembly until after the end of the specified period. In the case of the provisions dealing with fundamental rights this period will be the life of the first Parliament or four years from independence, whichever is the longer: in the case of the other provisions the specified period will be the life of the first two Parliaments or eight years from independence, whichever is the longer.

ANNEX B TRANSITIONAL CONSTITUTION AND RELATED LEGAL PROVISIONS

1   The Transitional Constitution will be contained in an Order in Council made under an Act of the United Kingdom Parliament. It will come into operation on a day to be appointed by the British Foreign and Commonwealth Secretary, and on that day Southern Rhodesia will return to legality.

The Residential Commissioner

2   The Transitional Constitution will establish the office of Resident Commissioner. The Resident Commissioner will be the representative of the Crown in Southern Rhodesia and in him will be vested responsibility for all executive and legislative functions of the Government of Southern Rhodesia. In exercising his functions, the Resident Commissioner will at all times be subject to any instructions that he may be given by the United Kingdom Government except so far as the Constitution otherwise expressly provides. The holder of the office of Resident Commissioner will be appointed and removable by the British Government. The Constitution will also establish the office of Deputy Resident Commissioner, the holder of which will similarly be appointed and removable by the British Government. The Deputy Resident Commissioner will generally assist the Resident Commissioner in his duties and will ordinarily act as Resident Commissioner if the latter has to be absent from Southern Rhodesia or is temporarily incapacitated. The Constitution will also provide for the emoluments of the Resident Commissioner and the Deputy Resident Commissioner and for the Resident Commissioner's staff.

Legislative powers

3   There will be no separate Legislative Assembly or other similar body during the transition period and, in its place, the Resident Commissioner will himself be the legislature. He will have full power to make laws for the peace, order and good government of Southern Rhodesia. This power will be exercisable by Ordinance signed by the Resident Commissioner and published in the

Official Gazette. All Ordinances made by the Resident Commissioner (and all subordinate legislation made under them or under any existing law) will be subject to the provisions of any applicable Act of the British Parliament or any Order in Council or other instrument made under such an Act and, in particular, will be subject to the provisions of the Transitional Constitution Order itself, especially the provisions of the Bill of Rights which will form part of the Transitional Constitution (see para. 8 below).

Executive powers

4 The Transitional Constitution will provide that the executive authority of Southern Rhodesia will be exercisable by the Resident Commissioner, as the representative of the Crown, either directly or through officers or authorities subordinate to him. Since there will be no Ministers during the transition period the Resident Commissioner will exercise all powers that are currently vested by any law in a Minister and he will, either directly or through officers subordinate to him, exercise supervision and control over all Ministries and departments of government. The Constitution will specifically give him power to give binding directions to all public officers and authorities.

5 The Resident Commissioner will be the Commander-in-Chief of all armed forces which may be lawfully operating in Southern Rhodesia during the transition period and, through the Commissioner of Police, he will also have ultimate command of the police forces. (References in this paragraph to armed forces do not include the United Nations Zimbabwe Force.) All members of all armed and police forces will be required to comply with the orders or directions given by the Resident Commissioner directly or through their superior officers. The Resident Commissioner will be empowered to require any member of any such force to swear an oath of allegiance to the Crown and an oath to uphold the Constitution and obey the laws of Southern Rhodesia. All powers relating to appointments in, disciplinary control over, and removal from office in any of these forces will be vested in the Resident Commissioner. Subject to any provision that he may make, they will be exercisable by the like authorities and in the like manner, as nearly as may be, as they

were immediately before the coming into operation of the Transitional Constitution but the exercise by those authorities of any such power will be subject to any general or special direction that the Resident Commissioner may give.

6 The Resident Commissioner will be able, if he considers it desirable, to set up one or more Advisory Councils or Committees to assist him in the performance of any specific function or of his functions generally. But he will be free to act without having consulted any such body or to act otherwise than in accordance with its advice if he does consult it.

Bill of Rights

7 The Transitional Constitution will contain a Bill of Rights (i.e. provisions guaranteeing fundamental human rights) on the lines of the one to be included in the Independence Constitution but adapted to take account of the fact that, during the transition period, the Resident Commissioner will take the place both of an elected legislature and of a Ministerial government. For a more detailed description of the rights to be guaranteed, see para. 5 (*a*) of Annex A.

8 Every law (whether an existing law that is continued in force during the transition period or a law made by the Resident Commissioner) will have to be read subject to the Bill of Rights and, if there is any conflict, will be invalid to the extent of the conflict. The Bill of Rights will be justiciable, i.e. any person who asserts that his rights under it have been, are being or are likely to be infringed by any law or by any government action will be able to apply to the High Court for that question to be determined and, when appropriate, for redress.

9 However, as in the case of the Bill of Rights in the Independence Constitution, there are two necessary qualifications to the position as described above:

(*a*) Some existing laws or administrative practices will be contrary to the Bill of Rights because they are discriminatory. It will be the intention of the Transitional Administration to abolish all discrimination, whether by legislation or by administrative practice, at as early a date as possible. However, it may be that some existing discriminatory laws or

administrative practices cannot simply be invalidated without
providing a new system to take their place, and that such new
system, or systems, will take some time to work out. Indeed,
in some cases it may be thought right that the task of creating
the new system should fall to the Government of Zimbabwe
and not be undertaken by the Transitional Administration.
In these limited cases, therefore, the Traditional Administration (and subsequently the Government of Zimbabwe: see
para. 5 (*c*) of Annex A) will be permitted to continue these
existing laws and practices, notwithstanding the Bill of
Rights, for such time as it takes to replace them but in any
case for no longer than two years from the date of independence.

(*b*) The Transitional Constitution (like the Independence Constitution) will permit certain of the provisions of the Bill of
Rights to be derogated from during period of public emergency. For this purpose, a public emergency will be recognised
as in existence whenever it has been proclaimed by the Resident Commissioner and until such time as he withdraws the
proclamation. As a precautionary measure, a number of the
emergency powers now operating in Southern Rhodesia will
need to be available to the Resident Commissioner immediately upon the commencement of the Transitional Constitution, which will therefore deem a proclamation of emergency
to be in force as from that date and until the Resident Commissioner himself otherwise provides. But it is the intention of the
British Government that this period of emergency should be
brought to an end as soon as it is prudent to do so and that, in
any event, the Resident Commissioner should take very early
steps to release existing detainees and also to release those
undergoing sentences of imprisonment for offences for which,
if proceedings had not already taken place, criminal liability
would be extinguished by the amnesty (see para. 18 (*c*) below).

Judicature

10   The Transitional Constitution will establish a High Court of
Southern Rhodesia staffed by a Chief Justice and other judges
and organised into a General Division and an Appellate Division

substantially as at present. It will also recognise such subordinate courts as are at present constituted under existing law.

11 The Transitional Constitution will provide that the judges of the High Court and the subordinate courts will be the persons who are serving in those respective capacities immediately before it comes into operation. (The office of Chief Justice, however, will be vacated by the present incumbent before the date of the return to legality and will not be filled until after that date.) Any new judge of the High Court will be appointed by the Resident Commissioner but a judge of the High Court, once appointed (and this includes such a judge who has been continued in office at the commencement of the Transitional Constitution), may not be removed until he reaches retiring age except for proved misconduct or incapacity, established by a judicial tribunal appointed by the Resident Commissioner. Nor can his terms of service be altered to his disadvantage during his tenure of office.

12 All powers relating to the appointment, disciplinary control and removal from office of the subordinate judiciary and the more senior staff of the High Court other than the judges (e.g. the Registrar) will be vested in the Resident Commissioner. Their exercise, subject to the overall control of the Resident Commissioner, by other persons and authorities in accordance with existing law will be regulated in the same way as for other offices in the public service (see para. 14 below).

13 During the transition period; appeals will lie from the High Court to the Judicial Committee of the Private Council but only by leave of the High Court or by special leave of the Judicial Committee.

The Public Service

14 All powers concerning appointments to offices in the public service, disciplinary control over persons holding or acting in such offices or their removal from office will be vested in the Resident Commissioner. Subject to any provision that he may make, they will be exercisable by the like authorities and in the like manner, as nearly as may be, as they were immediately before the coming into operation of the Transitional Constitution but the exercise by those authorities of any such power will

be subject to any general or special directions which the Resident Commissioner may give. The foregoing is without prejudice to the special provisions relating to the judges of the High Court (see para. 11 above).

15 The Transitional Constitution will provide that all persons holding or acting in public offices immediately before the coming into operation of the Constitution will continue to hold or act in the like offices under the Transitional Constitution. (There will, however, be a few offices, such as that of Secretary to the Cabinet, which will be vacated by the present incumbents before the date of the return to legality and will not be filled until after that date.) The Resident Commissioner will be empowered to require any person holding or acting in a public office to swear an oath of allegiance to the Crown and an oath to uphold the Constitution and observe the laws of Southern Rhodesia.

16 The pensions of all public officers (including past officers) will be guaranteed by the Transitional Constitution by:

    (i) being charged on the Consolidated Fund;
   (ii) a provision which will ensure that the pensions of officers who are compulsorily retired to facilitate the reconstruction of the public service can be freely remitted abroad, and
  (iii) a provision which will prevent the law regulating a public officer's pensions from being altered to his disadvantage after the commencement of his service.

Finance

17 The Transitional Constitution will contain provisions adapting the existing procedure for authorising the expenditure of public funds (e.g. annual Appropriation Acts.)

Miscellaneous provisions

18 In addition to the above matters which directly relate to the constitutional structure of the government of Southern Rhodesia during the transition period, there will be a number of other matters, necessarily consequential upon or incidental to the

restoration of legality, which will have to be regulated by the Transitional Constitution Order. The relevant provisions will include the following:

(a) *Validation of existing laws and previous transactions.* So that Southern Rhodesia may return to legality with a coherent and workable legal and administrative system, there will be a general validation of all laws which were purported to have been made during the period since 11 November 1965. There will be an exception for specified laws which would not be compatible with the restoration of legality, e.g. those relating to membership of the 'Parliament' that functioned during that period. Similarly, transactions which have taken place since 11 November 1965 and which might otherwise be regarded as invalid merely because they were carried out in reliance on any such law, or because (owing to the constitutional situation in Southern Rhodesia at the time) there was some defect in the authority by which they were performed or in the procedure employed or some other similar defect, will be deemed to have been validly performed.

(b) *Adaptation of existing laws.* A number of laws which will be in force on and after the day appointed for the coming into operation of the Transitional Constitution will be in terms which will not be literally applicable to the new constitutional arrangements. This will apply not only to laws made since 11 November 1965 which will have been validated as explained above but also to laws enacted by the competent legal authorities under the 1961 Constitution and indeed, earlier. For example, references in laws to 'the Minister' will no longer be appropriate. The reference will, during the transition period, have to be to 'the Resident Commissioner'. There will therefore be provision for the adaptation of existing laws to make them conform with the new constitutional structure.

(c) *Amnesty.* In order to bring to a close the unhappy chapter of the past 12 years and to open a new chapter which will be marked, it is hoped, by a spirit of reconciliation and the desire of all Rhodesians to work together for the construction of a peaceful and prosperous Zimbabwe, it will be necessary to 'wipe the slate clean' when legality is restored and to prevent punitive or recriminatory action being taken thereafter in respect of acts arising out of the political situation which obtained during that period. In practice it will be necessary to extinguish both civil and criminal liability for such acts. This applies to the acts of both sides, that is, both those committed in furtherance of the rebellion and those committed in resistance to it. The Transitional Constitution Order will therefore contain a provision to this end which will prevent prosecutions being brought or civil actions being pursued in the courts of Southern Rhodesia in respect of such acts. In addition, it will be a priority task of the Resident Commissioner to review the cases of all persons undergoing imprisonment and to order the immediate release of those serving sentences for offences for which, if proceedings had not already taken place, criminal liability would be extinguished by this provision.

(*d*) *Rights and liabilities of the Government of Southern Rhodesia.* The Transitional Constitution Order will make it clear, for the avoidance of doubt, that the Government of Southern Rhodesia, as set up by that Order, is entitled to all the rights, and is subject to all the obligations, now appertaining to the Government of Southern Rhodesia as set up by the 1961 Constitution. Furthermore, as a corollary of the provision explained above for the validation of existing laws and of past transactions, it will also be expressly declared that the lawful Government of Southern Rhodesia, as established by the Transitional Constitution, will succeed at the same time to the rights and assets (and, correspondingly, to the obligations) in municipal law which would, immediately before the coming into operation of that Constitution, have been recognised by the courts then operating in Southern Rhodesia as belonging to 'the Government of the Republic of Rhodesia'.

ANNEX C   THE ZIMBABWE DEVELOPMENT FUND

1   A political settlement in Rhodesia, involving first a transitional administration and later an independent Government of Zimbabwe, would remove a source of acute conflict and help establish a climate conducive to economic development in central and southern Africa. A political settlement, however, will set in motion an economic transition which will be most effective if

accompanied by measures designed to realise the growth potential of the economy and rapidly improve opportunities for all the population of Zimbabwe. The responsibility for the necessary economic measures after independence will rest primarily with the new Government, but it is already evident in spite of the sparse detail at present available about the present state and future prospects of the economy, that substantial international economic assistance, and external private investment will be needed.

2 When a political settlement is achieved, the lifting of sanctions, combined with aid, will provide both Zimbabwe and its neighbours with new development prospects. Different trade and transport patterns will be established. African Zimbabweans should have expanded access to better jobs in mining, industry, commerce and the public service. More balanced patterns of ownership for farms, houses, and businesses will emerge. External assistance can help the people of Zimbabwe effect the social and economic changes required to take advantage of these new opportunities for a more prosperous and balanced economy.

3 The ability of an independent Government of Zimbabwe to raise the living standards of the poor majority depends not only on the development of the traditional sector but also on effective administration and a high level of output in the modern sector, which accounts for the greater part of Rhodesia's export earnings, internal revenues, domestic production of consumer goods, and wage employment of African Zimbabweans. It is, therefore, of the greatest importance to find ways to facilitate the economic transition while minimising its disruptive effect on the potential for economic growth. It is crucial that skilled workers and managerial personnel are encouraged to continue to contribute to the welfare and prosperity of the economy.

4 The United Kindom and the United States have, therefore, agreed to co-operate in helping to organise an international economic effort in support of a Rhodesian settlement. They propose the establishment of a Zimbabwe Development Fund. The purpose of this Fund would be to assist the new government to promote:

  (i) balanced economic and social development in Zimbabwe;
  (ii) rapid expansion of economic opportunities for and skills of the African majority;

(iii) basic economic security for all sections of the population so that they might continue to contribute their skills and enthusiasm to the development of the country.

5 The Fund would respond to requests from the Zimbabwe Government to support specific proposals for development projects and programmes, for example, in agricultural and land reform, education and training, and social and economic infrastructure. Its efforts should encourage commercial capital flows, especially in extractive, processing, and manufacturing industries, supported as appropriate by national export credit and investment insurance agencies. The Fund should be prepared to provide balance of payments support during the period of economic transition, especially to enable the gradual return to normal external relations after the lifting of sanctions. The Fund could also provide support for, and take into account the balance of payments implications of, programmes designed to encourage skilled labour and managerial personnel to contribute to Zimbabwe development and to effect a smooth transition to a more balanced pattern of access to ownership of farms, houses, and businesses.

6 The Fund should be established as soon as possible after the establishment of a transitional administration in Rhodesia. Even before it began to be funded to any considerable extent, the Fund could begin working with developmental institutions, either already existing or to be established by the Zimbabwe Government. The Fund could assist both the transitional administration and the independent Government of Zimbabwe to plan development projects and programmes consistent with the political changes which will have taken place without disruption of the economy. The Fund could, in the initial period, also co-ordinate bilateral development assistance, especially in the training of Africans in technical and administrative skills.

7 Since specific development projects and programmes for an independent Zimbabwe are not available, a precise quantification of the resources needed by the Fund is not possible. A preliminary assessment, however, suggests that the target for total contributions, on concessionary terms from those Governments willing to participate in the Fund should be at a minimum approaching US$1000 million and at a maximum rather less than US$1500 million. The Fund's objectives, and the fact that ex-

perience shows that economic development projects take a long time to mature, will make it necessary to envisage a fairly long period of disbursement of a Fund's resources. It is suggested, however, in order that the management of the Fund can plan its operations in the knowledge of the total amount of its resources and so that it can meet extraordinary balance of payments demands on its resources during an economic transition, that contributions by participating Governments should be made over a five-year period with the likelihood of a longer period of actual disbursement in mind.

8 Flows of bilaterial concessional aid could, it is suggested, be counted as part of their contribution to the Fund, but the greater part of each country's contribution, at least during the first five years of its operation, should be direct to the Fund. On this basis, initial finance envisaged for the Fund might be, say, two-thirds over a five-year period in cash or in promissory notes, and, say, one-third on call if the management of the Fund should require it for the fulfilment of its longer-term objectives. The method by which the contributions were made can be discussed between Governments and need not necessarily be uniform. For example, some Governments might prefer to contribute cash at regular intervals in equal instalments. Others might prefer to make available promissory notes for encashment as disbursements by the Fund require, a method permitted in replenishment of the resources of the International Development Association. The questions of the currencies in which contributions should be made, the degree and structure of any arrangement for tying of procurement in the participating countries and provision for the local costs of development projects can be the subject of intergovernmental consultation. The nature of the economic assistance extended by the Fund should be such that the contributions of participating Governments would be expected to qualify as official development assistance in accordance with the criteria of the Development Assistance Committee.

9 On this basis, the Government of the United Kingdom would be prepared, subject to Parliamentary approval, to contribute 15 per cent of the resources provided directly to the Fund, up to a maximum of £75 million, and in addition to provide £41 million of bilateral aid over a five-year period; and the Government of the United States would, subject to the authorisation and appropriation of funds by Congress, be prepared to contribute 40 per

cent to the total resources of the Fund, up to a maximum of $520 million, the major part a direct contribution to the Fund and the rest in the form of bilateral assistance. The British and United States contributions would be conditional on each other and on contributions being forthcoming from other countries on an equitable basis.

10 The fund will also facilitate action by agencies of donor countries to make appropriate non-concessional loans and guarantees to encourage commercial trade and private investment flows to Zimbabwe. These would be additional to the concessionary contributions discussed above. The Fund could also provide support for regional development projects and take part in any consortium or consultative group established to co-ordinate development assistance to Zimbabwe and relate it to development aid to the Southern Africa region as a whole.

11 It is envisaged that the World Bank would manage the Fund's resources as an agent of the Fund. Matters of policy would be discussed and decided by a governing body, which might be composed of the IBRD Executive Directors representing the Governments contributing to the Fund, together with representation from the Zimbabwe Government.

SOURCE AND NOTE Cmnd Paper 6919 ('Rhodesia: Proposals for a Settlement') reproduced herein is Crown copyright 1977 and is reprinted by permission of the Controller of Her Majesty's Stationery Office.

With regard to Annex 3, 'The Zimbabwe Development Fund', note that, when the US proposed a $1500 million development fund aimed at aiding the economy of the new Zimbabwean state, it was thought that this fund would be used to buy out white landowners. Since whites own most of the food land in the country, it naturally followed that land reform would be necessary. Western governments also hoped that Bishop Muzorewa would win the prime ministership and therefore 'by-pass' the $1500 million United States fund. However, since the election of Robert Mugabe, the other Western nations are claiming that their national economies are in a state of crisis and that they are therefore unable to fulfil the proposed commitment.

Notes

NOTES TO CHAPTER ONE. THE ANDREW YOUNG AFFAIR REVISITED

1. *Brown* vs *Board of Education* (Topeka, Kan).
2. This allegation grew out of FBI covert operations authorised by then Attorney General, Robert F. Kennedy. These operations, directed by the late J. Edgar Hoover, contrived incriminating evidence against Civil Rights activists.
3. Mark Lane and Dick Gregory, *Code Name 'Zorro': The Murder of Martin Luther King, Jr* (New York: Pakangaroo, 1977) p. 95.
4. Ibid., p. 115
5. Ibid.
6. Ibid., p. 72. Young previously sought the Congressional post in 1970.
7. Gerald Bennett was formerly an Assistant Professor of Sociology at Memphis State University. He is currently Tennessee State Chairperson of the Citizen's Party and a doctoral candidate at Michigan State University at Lansing.
8. Tony Brown, 'Atlanta Racist Like Rest of US', *Mid-South Express News Service* (Memphis: Tenn.), 11–17 Nov 1981, p. 8.
9. Ibid.
10. Ibid.
11. Derrick Bell, 'Learning from the Brown Experience', *Black Scholar*, vol. II, no. 1 (Sep–Oct 1979) pp. 10–12.
12. Lu Palmer, 'Andrew Young Has a Lot of Black Folks Worried', *Black Book Bulletin* (Institute of Positive Education, Chicago), Spring (no year).
13. Mark Allen, 'James E. Carter and the Trilateral Commission', *Black Scholar*, vol. 8, no. 7 (May 1977) p. 2. Carter's reputation amongst the transnational bourgeoisie is predicated on his record as Governor of Georgia. While in this post he opened trade offices linking the state of Georgia to Brussels and Tokyo.
14. This kind of thinking coupled with the Reagan Administration's decision to join forces with its Caribbean allies and invade Grenada in October 1983 proves a continuity of policy and practice in US foreign relations which cuts across party lines.
15. Allen, in *Black Scholar*, vol. 8, no. 7, p. 6.
16. Ibid., p. 2.
17. Matthew Holden Jr, *The Politics of the Black 'Nation'* (New York: Chandler, 1973) p. 42.
18. Llewellyn is a Percy Sutton/Leon Sullivan type black businessman from

New York. Percy Sutton is the former President of the Borough of Manhattan in New York. The former air-force intelligence officer earned national recognition for his skilful handling of urban problems. Now out of politics, he is chairman of the Inner City Broadcasting Company, which owns radio stations in New York, Detroit and California. Sutton's group plans to enter the cable television business and also plans to refurbish the famous Apollo Theatre in Harlem to air entertainment via cable television. The Reverend Leon Sullivan is the founder and board chairman of the Opportunities Industrialization Centers of America (OIC). He was a prominent participant in A. Philip Randolph's successful threat to march on Washington to obtain jobs for blacks. Sullivan served as an aide to Adam Clayton Powell Jr during Powell's campaign for congressman. In Philadelphia, in 1964 Sullivan formed OIC, which soon became one of the largest and most prestigious job training operations in the world. Sullivan was named a director of General Motors in 1971. He is the author of the *Sullivan Principles*, the guidelines for firms investing in South Africa.

19. See Andrew Young, 'A New Kind of Teamwork', *Topic*, no. 126 (1979) pp. 2–4.
20. The UPE scheme became outdated when the policy of public-sponsored education was expanded beyond the primary-school level. The free-education mandate which swept the country between 1978 and 1983, particularly in the south, presented state governments with an even greater demand for textbooks, because the new free-education movement called for publicly sponsored education at the primary, secondary and higher education levels. Booksellers were among the significant beneficiaries of the new free-education mandate. Today, free education is no longer extended to higher education, this being a result of the economic crisis of Nigeria. S. O. Awokoya is credited with being the father of free education in Nigeria.
21. Holden, *Politics of the Black 'Nation'*, p. 43.
22. See Young, *Topic*, no. 126, p. 3.
23. See transcribed version of televised dialogue with Young on *America's Black Forum*, a syndicated television programme. Also cited by Lu Palmer in *Black Book Bulletin*, Spring (no year) p. 29.
24. Though we do not personally hold the view that these twenty seats could have any significant power, when the proposal was conceived it was believed by those who made it that these twenty seats were a major step toward forming a white power base in a black-ruled Zimbabwe. With the Parliament dominated by the Zimbabwe African National Union (ZANU) and the Zimbabwe African Peoples' Union (ZAPU), the power of these seats would have been virtually nil.
25. The Nigerian regime supported the Anglo–American plan as a means of keeping favour with the United States. Nigeria later withdrew her support.
26. Manning Marable gives examples of the compromise between the Tuskegee ruling class and Johnny Ford, the black neocolonial mayor of Tuskegee. The compromise involves the black petit-bourgeoisie exploiting Federal funds and the local white ruling class continuing to exploit and control Tuskegee's economic base. The black lay public, on

the other hand, faces the dual problem of unemployment and inflation. The concept of deference politics (resurrected from the works of V. O. Keys) provides the theoretical thread informing Marable's political critique. See 'Tuskegee, Alabama: The Politics of Illusion in the New South', *Black Scholar*, vol. 8, no. 7 (May 1977) pp. 13–24.

27. Charles V. Hamilton, 'The 80's Politics', *Ebony*, Jan 1980, p. 36.
28. Ibid.
29. Ibid.
30. See Yusufu Bala Usman, *For the Liberation of Nigeria* (London: New Beacon, 1979) pp. 177–8. See also the records of the US Senate Foreign Relations Committee, 24 July 1975. This document provides a detailed history of the US role in the military build-up in South Africa.
31. On 4 March 1980, however, Robert Mugabe was elected to power in Zimbabwe. According to the BBC (Radio), Mugabe called for a coalition government with Joshua Nkomo. Mugabe's foreign policy is a nonaligned one. Zimbabwe would have diplomatic relations with those countries who are against apartheid in South Africa. Mugabe appointed Joshua Nkomo Home Affairs Minister, thereby placing him in charge of the Zimbabwean Police Force. Mugabe's cabinet consists of twenty-two members, two of whom are white and four of whom belong to ZAPU, the party led by Nkomo. Since 1980 there have been internal conflicts in the Zimbabwean government, resulting in the dismissal of Joshua Nkomo from political office.
32. Palmer, in *Black Book Bulletin*, Spring (no year) p. 29.
33. Young said that it was better to establish relations through the leadership of Neto and Machel than to deal with even more radical personalities among the leftist rank and file in Southern Africa. See Western Massachusetts Association of Concerned African Scholars, *US Military Involvement in Southern Africa* (Dar es Salaam: Tanzania Publishing; and Boston, Mass.: South End Press, 1978) pp. 48–9.

    The situation which prompted Andrew Young to express his opinion of MPLA and Cuban–Soviet influence in Angola was, first, the international concern for Soviet–Cuban influence in Africa; and, second, the continuing border dispute between Angola and Zaire, which was caused by the movement of FNLA rebels across the border between the two states. Historically, Zaire had been a stronghold for FNLA troops; in fact, all of Angola's liberation organisations used Zaire as a base during the period of Portuguese rule. In 1975, 100 Chinese guerrilla-instructors were sent to Zaire to train FNLA troops. Since the Cubans and Soviets backed the MPLA, China, contemptuous of the USSR and Cuba, decided to support the FNLA. China later withdrew from the area when FNLA and UNITA forces became involved with South Africa.
34. *African Contemporary Record: Annual Survey of Documents 1975–1976*, ed. Colin Legum (London: Rex Collings, 1976) p. B432.
35. Ibid., p. B433. Gulf's $500 million in taxes and royalties paid to the People's Republic of Angola constituted 60 per cent of the country's annual national revenue.
36. *Africa Contemporary Record: Annual Survey and Documents 1976–1977*, ed. Colin Legum (London: Rex Collings, 1977) p. B458.

37. Ibid., p. B447. In 1974 and 1975 several black nationalist organisations in the United States threw their support behind Jonus Savimbi and UNITA. However, by 1976, when it became clear UNITA was being backed by South Africa and the CIA, black nationalists, with the exception of the infamous Congress of Racial Equality (CORE), withdrew their support from the UNITA faction and recognised the MPLA as the legitimate government and popular liberation front in Angola. Since the middle 1970s CORE, under the directorship of Roy Innis, has been suspect in the national and international scene.

38. It is believed that the USSR and Cuba intervened in Angola to stop a counter-revolution after learning a hard lesson in Chile, Greece and Indonesia. There is a pattern in the Soviet–Cuban approach which can be seen in Angola, Ethiopia, Afghanistan and Poland.

39. Mohammed El-Khawas and Barry Cohen, *The Kissinger Study of Southern Africa: National Security Study Memorandum 39* (Westport, Conn: Lawrence Hill, 1976) p. 84. For option 2, see pp. 105–9.

40. *Apartheid Quiz* (London: International Defence and Aid Fund, 1976) p. 51.

41. Quoted by Mark Allen in *Black Scholar*, vol. 8, no. 7, p. 7.

42. Young made this assertion in South Africa during his visit there in January 1977. See Phyllis P. Jordon, 'The Apartheid System: Its Economic Dimensions', paper presented to Afro-American Museum Seminar on South Africa, Southgate, Mich., 4 June 1977, p. 12. See also 'Andrew Young and US Neocolonial Designs', *Southern Africa News* (Washington, DC), vol. 1, no. 2 (June 1977) pp. 2–4. In Jordon's paper one can see how Young promotes non-violence and integration, while at the same time making the African situation a hegemony with white businessmen in control. In January 1977 Young met with 100 businessmen and industrialists in South Africa. The affair was arranged by mining-tycoon, Harry Oppenheimer.

43. In these arrangements national resources are either exploited or under-developed. Recently, in Nigeria, indigenous chicken farmers were being threatened by frozen imported chickens from the United States and Western Europe (*Daily Times*, 5 Feb 1980, pp. 16–17). Such arrangements call for strict control by the governments of the so-called developing nations.

44. See *Ebony*, Dec 1979, p. 42.

45. In addition to its ties to Gulf Oil, the Angolan government is permitting a conglomeration of French, Belgian and American oil companies to explore for oil along Angola's coastline. If oil is discovered in the area, the participating oil companies will be allowed to buy and export the oil (BBC World Service to Africa, 4 Sep 1980). The problem with pragmatic socialism, as it is practised today, is its potential to become state capitalism.

46. See 'An Awkward Time to Leave Ghana', *West Africa* (London), 29 June 1981, p. 1462.

47. Ibid.

48. Ibid., p. 1463.

49. Ibid., p. 1462.

50. Ibid.
51. Ibid.
52. Ibid., p. 1463
53. Ibid., p. 1462
54. See cover story of *Newsweek*, 3 Sep 1979.
55. See *The Universal Jewish Encyclopedia*, vol. 14 (1941) s.v. 'Elders of Zion', p. 58.
56. *Africa Contemporary Record: Annual Survey of Documents 1978–1979*, ed. Colin Legum (London and New York: Africana, 1980) p. B923.
57. Ibid.
58. Ibid.
59. Ibid.
60. When campaigning in the mayoral election in Atlanta, Young spoke of offsetting the city's economic problems by linking the Atlanta business sector with the African, Middle East and Caribbean business sectors. After becoming mayor, Young began negotiating an agreement with Nigeria Airways and the Nigerian government for direct flights from Lagos to Atlanta. This business proposal is purely romantic, because the drastic drop in Nigeria's oil sales (1981–2) has affected Nigeria Airways' operations. With the airline operating out of a deficit, Nigeria Airways is now struggling to maintain its existing flights. There is little reason to be optimistic about the airline expanding its operations. See Andrew Young, 'Economic Development', *Ivy Leaf*, Fall 1982, pp. 9–11.
61. Marcel Liebman, *The Russian Revolution* (New York: Vintage Books, 1970) p. 342.

NOTES TO CHAPTER TWO. THE CIA: COVERT OPERATIONS IN
SOUTHERN AFRICA, WITH SPECIAL REFERENCE TO ANGOLA

1. See *The Pentagon Papers*, ed. M. Gravel (Boston, Mass.: Beacon Press, 1971) ch. 1.
2. US Senate, *Select Committee to Study Government Operations with Respect to Intelligence Activities, Alleged Assassination Plots Involving Foreign Leaders: Interim Report*, 94th Congress, 1st session (Washington, DC: Government Printing Office, 1975) p. 14.
3. John Stockwell, *In Search of Enemies: A CIA Story* (New York: Norton, 1978) pp. 105, 160 n. and 201 n.
4. The 'imperialist powers' here means Britain, France, the Federal Republic of Western Germany and Portugal.
5. For details see 'History of the Central Intelligence Agency', in US Senate, *Supplementary Detailed Staff Reports on Foreign and Military Intelligence*, vol. IV, 94th Congress, 2nd Session (Washington, DC: Government Printing Office, 1976) p. 68.
6. What Jonas Savimbi could not achieve (and his achievements are still open to question) during his visit to Washington shortly after the installation of Ronald Reagan, is being pursued in the US Senate. The *Sunday New Nigerian*, 26 July 1981, published a brief news release

stating, 'African members of the United Nations have protested against moves in the United States Senate to repeal a prohibition on overt or covert United States military aid or activity in Angola. They said in a statement that there was a danger that this was aimed at stepping up American intervention in Angola, in an attempt to destabilise its legitimate government. The African members said that a repeal of the legislation, known as the Clark Amendment, would strengthen South Africa's military capability for its "continuous acts of aggression", against Angola, which borders Namibia.'

7. *The CIA and the Cult of Intelligence*, ed. Victor Marchetti and John Marks (New York: Alfred Knopf, 1974) pp. 380–98.
8. Philip Agee, *Inside the Company: A CIA Diary* (London: Stonehill, 1975) pp. 46–50.
9. *The CIA and the Cult of Intelligence*, pp. 386–9.
10. Ibid., p. 387.
11. Ibid., p. 386.
12. Ibid., p. 391.
13. See 'The Pike Reports', in *Village Voice* (New York), 16 Feb 1976 pp. 83–84.
14. *The CIA and the Cult of Intelligence*, pp. 69–70.
15. *Washington Post* (Washington, DC), 26 May 1973, p. 5.
16. *The CIA and the Cult of Intelligence*, p. 392.
17. Stockwell, *In Search of Enemies*, pp. 169 and 201.
18. *The CIA and the Cult of Intelligence*, p. 63.
19. Morton Halperin, 'Covert Operations – Effects of Secrecy on Decision-Making', in *The CIA File*, ed. R. Borosage and John Marks (New York: Grossman, 1976) pp. 1–15.
20. Stockwell, *In Search of Enemies*, p. 105.
21. 'History of the Central Intelligence Agency', in US Senate, *Select Committee to Study Government Operations with Respect to Intelligence Activities . . . Interim Report.*
22. Ibid.
23. Agee, *Inside the Company*, p. 54.
24. Ibid.
25. See the series of articles by Robert Moss in the *Sunday Telegraph* (London), 23 Jan–20 Feb 1977.
26. Stockwell, *In Search of Enemies*, pp. 181 and 220–1.
27. Agee, *Inside the Company*.
28. Tad Szulk, *The Illusion of Peace: Foreign Policy in the Nixon Years* (New York: Viking, 1978) pp. 224–5.
29. Ibid.
30. See *International Defence and Aid for Southern Africa. Boss: The First Five Years* (London: Stonehill, 1975) chs 1 and 2.
31. *Daily Telegraph* (London), 26 July 1969, p. 7.
32. Stockwell, *In Search of Enemies*, pp. 187–8.
33. See William Colby, *Honorable Men: My Life in the CIA* (New York: Simon and Schuster, 1978) p. 286.
34. The Portuguese Secret Police – the Direccaõ Geral de Seguranca (DGS)

is one of the oldest Western secret intelligence agencies. The DGS originated in 1920s as Salazar's political police. In the 1930s it received advice and training from Hitler's Gestapo and Mussolini's Opera Volontaria Repressione Antifascismo (OVRA). For a brief history of the DGS, see de Oliviera Marques, *History of Portugal*, 2nd edn (New York: Columbia University Press, 1976) pp. 187–8.

35. K. Maxwell, 'Portugal under Pressure', in *New York Review of Books*, 29 May 1978, p. 3.
36. *New York Times*, 25 Sep 1975, p. 5.
37. El-Khawas and Cohen, *The Kissinger Study of Southern Africa*, p. 28.
38. *Village Voice*, 16 Feb 1976, p. 79.
39. *Race to Power* (Boston, Mass.: Africa Research Group, 1969) pp. 50–75.
40. Colby, *Honorable Men*, p. 387.
41. See column by Evans and Novak in the *Washington Post*, 25 Feb 1977, p. 16.
42. Leopold Laufer, *Israel and the Developing Countries: New Approaches to Cooperation* (New York: Twentieth Century Fund, 1968) p. 47.
43. For details see Ray Schaap *et al., Dirty Work: The CIA in Africa* (Secaucus, NJ: Lyle Stuart, 1979) pp. 46–50.
44. Ibid.
45. Stockwell, *In Search of Enemies*, p. 67.
46. Tad Szulk, 'Lisbon and Washington: Behind the Portuguese Revolution', *Foreign Policy*, no. 21 (Winter 1975–6) p. 33.
47. Moss, in *Sunday Telegraph*, 23 Jan – 20 Feb 1977.
48. *Africa Contemporary Record: Annual Survey of Documents 1974–1975*, ed. Colin Legum (London: Rex Collings, 1975) p. B536.
49. *New York Times*, 11 June 1974, p. 7.
50. Stockwell, *In Search of Enemies*, p. 258.
51. John Stockwell, interview with O. Abegunrin, Washington, DC, May 1978.
52. Rene Lemarchand, *American Policy in Southern Africa: The Stakes and the Stance* (Washington, DC: University Press of America, 1978) p. 76.
53. Stockwell, *In Search of Enemies*, p. 67 n.
54. Ibid.
55. Ibid., p. 68.
56. Ibid.
57. See *Der Spiegel* (Bonn, West Germany, 19 Aug 1975) pp. 3–4.
58. Ibid.
59. Szulk, in *Foreign Policy*, no. 21, p. 29.
60. Ibid., pp. 29–30.
61. Stockwell, *In Search of Enemies*, pp. 67–8.
62. Ibid., pp. 63–4.
63. US House of Representatives, *Special Sub-Committee of House International Relations, Hearing on Mercenaries in Africa*, 94th Congress, 2nd Session (Washington, DC: Government Printing Office, 1976) p. 42.
64. Stockwell, *In Search of Enemies*, pp. 58–9.
65. Ibid., p. 158.

66. Lemarchand, *American Policy in Southern Africa*, p. 83.
67. US House of Representatives, *Special Sub-Committee . . . Hearing on Mercenaries*, p. 49.
68. Stockwell, *In Search of Enemies*, p. 168.
69. Ibid., p. 177.
70. US House of Representatives, *Special Sub-Committee . . . Hearing on Mercenaries*, p. 47.
71. '20 Russians and 35 Cubans Captured by UNITA in Angola', *Washington Post*, 22 Nov 1975, pp. 1 and 6.
72. Stockwell, *In Search of Enemies*, pp. 187–8.
73. *Washington Post*, 18–30 Sep 1975.
74. *Extra-ordinary Summit Conference of the OAU, Held in Addis-Ababa, Ethiopia, January 10–11, 1976* (Lagos: Ministry of Information, Jan 1976) pp. 1–9.
75. Michael Getler, 'Senate Repealed the So-Called Hughes–Ryan Amendment', *Washington Post*, 23 Mar 1980, p. 1.
76. Michael Getler, 'Senate Votes to End Curb on Covert Aid in Angola', *Washington Post*, 24 June 1980, pp. 1 and 8.
77. Ibid.

NOTES TO CHAPTER THREE. THE CARTER ADMINISTRATION'S POLICY ON SOUTHERN AFRICA, 1977–80

1. See option 2 of National Security Study Memorandum 39; full text in El-Khawas and Cohen, *The Kissinger Study of Southern Africa*, p. 106.
2. Ibid.
3. Ibid.
4. Ibid.
5. 'US President Elect, Jimmy Carter', *Financial Mail* (Johannesburg), 3 Nov 1976, p. 1.
6. 'Mr Young's Fact-Finding Trip to Nigeria and Southern Africa', *Daily Times* (Lagos), 10 Feb 1977, p. 1.
7. Michael Getler, 'The Change in Carter's Foreign Policy', *Washington Post*, 3 June 1978, p. 5.
8. An address by Secretary of State Cyrus Vance before the Annual Convention of the National Association for the Advancement of Colored People (NAACP), St Louis, Missouri, July 1977, pp. 1–4.
9. Ibid.
10. Ralph Uwechue, 'Interview with Andrew Young', *Africa* (London), no. 71, July 1977, pp. 11–16.
11. Zimbabwe became independent at midnight on 17 April 1980, with Robert Mugabe as Prime Minister. See Jay Ross, 'The Birth of Zimbabwe', *Washington Post*, 18 Apr 1980, p. 1.
12. *Washington Post*, May 1977, p. 5.
13. John de St Jorre, *A House Divided: South Africa's Uncertain Future* (Washington, DC: Carnegie Endowment for International Peace, 1977) p. 128.

14. *Daily Times* (Lagos), 10 Feb 1977, pp. 1–2.
15. See *Washington Notes on Africa* (Washington, DC: Washington Office on Africa, Spring 1978) pp. 1–4.
16. The all-party talks on the Namibian independence settlement were held in Geneva from 7 to 14 January 1981. The conference eventually broke down because the South African delegation, led by Danie Hough, refused to accept the UN election plan, unless the United Nations confessed its bias and changed its ways, renouncing all support for SWAPO, or at least giving equal support and recognition to the Democratic Turnhalle Alliance. For details, see Jane Coles, 'Namibia: The Geneva Charade', *Africa*, no. 114, (Feb 1981) pp. 22–5; and 'SWAPO Spurs South Africa On', *Daily Sketch* (Nigeria), 12 Jan 1981, p. 12.
17. *Washington Post*, 10 Feb 1977, p. 1.
18. Ibid.
19. *Rhodesia: Proposals for a Settlement* (London: Her Majesty's Stationery Office, Sep 1977).
20. Joshua Nkomo, interview with O. Abegunrin, Washington, DC, 18 June 1978.
21. 'US–African Policy Under Carter', *Africa*, no. 106 (June 1980) p. 83.
22. John Stockwell, 'What Should be the Role of the CIA in US Policy in Africa', in *AEI, Foreign Policy and Defense Review* (Washington, DC), vol. 1. no. 1 (1979) p. 65.
23. Getler, *Washington Post*, 3 May 1977, p. 9.
24. Ibid.
25. Ernest Harsch and Tony Thomas, *Angola: The Hidden History of Washington's War* (New York: Pathfinder, 1976) pp. 97–108.
26. *Washington Post*, 10 Nov 1979, p. 2.
27. Richard Nixon, *The Real War* (New York: Warner, 1980) pp. 9–12.
28. Andrew Young, 'An End to "Carte Blanche" in South Africa', *Washington Post*, 24 June 1980, p. 11.
29. Henry Kissinger, *White House Years, 1969–1973* (Boston, Mass.: Little, Brown, 1979) p. 129.
30. Ibid., pp. 129–34.

NOTES TO CHAPTER FOUR. NIGERIA, SOUTH AFRICA AND THE US CONNECTION: MYTH AND THE WESTERN-PROCLAIMED 'GIANT OF AFRICA'

1. *Nigerian Government and Politics Under Military Rule 1976–1979*, ed. Oyeleye Oyediran (London: Macmillan, 1979) p. 155.
2. Speech by the Nigerian Commissioner for Industry at the opening of the National Conference on 'Nigeria and the World', held at the Nigerian Institute of International Affairs, Lagos, 27 Jan 1976.
3. '₦ 13 million for MPLA', *West Africa*, no. 3053 (5 Jan 1976) p. 22.
4. 'Shameless America', editorial in *Nigerian Daily Sketch* (Ibadan), 8 Jan 1976, p. 2.
5. *New Nigerian* (Kaduna), Sep 15 1975, p. 14.

6. 'Nigeria Recognizes the African National Congress (ANC) of Zimbabwe', *Daily Times* (Lagos), 1 Dec 1975, p. 1.
7. *Africa Research Bulletin* (London), July 1976, p. 4080.
8. 'Rhodesian Talks', *West Africa*, no. 3095 (25 Oct 1976) p. 1602.
9. David Sibeku, leader of the Pan-African Congress of South Africa, visited Nigeria in 1976. See *West Africa*, no. 3088 (6 Sep 1976) p. 1305.
10. 'President Kaunda in Nigeria', *West Africa*, no. 3107 (24 Jan 1977) p. 173.
11. 'Police Have Questioned a European and two Nigerian Managers of a Major Department Store', *West Africa*, no. 3111 (21 Feb 1977) p. 390.
12. See *West Africa*, no. 3088.
13. 'Nigeria's Support for Liberation of Continent', *Nigeria Review*, no. 8 (Lagos: Federal Ministry of Information, June 1977) pp. 1–2.
14. Ibid.
15. The Sullivan Principles, named after their author, a member of General Motors board of directors, have been urged by the US government officials and accepted by the South African government as guidelines for US firms investing in South Africa. See Ann Seidman, 'Why US Corporations Should Get out of South Africa', *Issue*, vol. x, nos 1 and 2 (Spring–Summer, 1980) p. 81.
16. Young, 'A New Kind of Teamwork', speech delivered before the Nigerian–American Chamber of Commerce, Sep 1979, in *Topic*, no. 126, p. 3.
17. See *Africa Contemporary Record: Annual Survey of Documents 1978–1979*, p. B920.
18. David C. Martin and John Walcott, 'Smuggling Arms to South Africa', *Washington Post*, 5 Aug 1979, p. B1.
19. *Africa Contemporary Record: Annual Survey of Documents 1979–1980*, ed. Colin Legum (London and New York: Africana, 1980) pp. B862–863.
20. Ibid., p. B864. In 1978 Britain exported to Nigeria twice as much as to South Africa. British exports to South Africa were valued at R1200 million. See *Africa Contemporary Record: Annual Survey of Documents 1979–1980*, p. B864.
21. For details see 'No Compromise with Apartheid', *The World Conference for Action against Apartheid* (Lagos: Federal Ministry of Information, 1977) pp. 1–2.
22. *News Release*, 22 Aug 1977 (Lagos: Federal Ministry of Information) p. 2.
23. Ibid.
24. J. N. Garba's address to the UN Security Council Meeting on 'The Namibian Question', *Nigeria in the UN 1975–1976* (New York: Nigerian Permanent Mission to the UNO, 1976) p. 9.
25. See *Africa Contemporary Record: Annual Survey of Documents 1976–1977*, p. B681.
26. *Forbes* (New York), vol. 7, no. 162 (Dec 1977) p. 18.
27. *News Release no. 386* (Lagos: Federal Ministry of Information, Mar 1976) p. 14.
28. General Obasanjo, 'Summit of Unity', speech delivered at the 14th

Summit Conference of the OAU, held in Libreville, Gabon (Lagos: Calmen Press, 1977) p. 9.

29. Olajide Aluko, 'Nigeria, US and Southern Africa', *African Affairs*, vol. 78, no. 310 (Jan 1979) p. 94.
30. *Sunday Sketch* (Ibadan), 10 June 1977, p. 16.
31. 'Obasanjo Addresses UN', *West Africa*, no. 3146 (24 Oct 1977) p. 2180.
32. 'Obasanjo for US', *West Africa*, no. 3141 (19 Sep 1977) p. 1953.
33. Muhammed Haruna, 'Obasanjo's Visit to US: Some Reflections', *New Nigerian* (Kaduna), 21 Oct 1977, p. 15.
34. *Africa Contemporary Record: Annual Survey of Documents 1977–1978*, ed. Colin Legum (London ,and New York: Africana, 1979) pp. B750–1.
35. 'President Carter Sends Message to Foreign Audience', *News Release*, 21 Jan 1977 (Ibadan: USIS Cocoa House) p. 1.
36. A. B. Akinyemi, 'Re-ordering Nigeria's Foreign Policy' (public lecture delivered at the Club de Capital, University of Ibadan, Jan 1978) p. 3.
37. Bala Usman, 'Nigeria's South African Policy Today – The Subservience to America', *New Nigerian*, 15 Oct 1977, p. 5.
38. Aluko, in *African Affairs*, vol. 78, no. 310, pp. 94–5.
39. *Daily Times* (Lagos), 13 Apr 1977, p. 3.
40. 'Brigadier Garba's Annual Report', *New Nigerian*, 14 Feb 1978, p. 1.
41. Aluko, in *African Affairs*, vol. 78, no. 310, p. 95.
42. Ibid.
43. *Daily Times*, 20 Jan 1979, p. 32.
44. *Daily Times*, 24 Dec 1977, p. 6.
45. Aluko, in *African Affairs*, vol. 78, no. 310, p. 97.

NOTES TO CHAPTER FIVE. SOUTHERN AFRICA AND THE REAGAN
ADMINISTRATION

1. For details, see 'Crocker Memorandum of Pretoria Meeting', *Sunday New Nigerian*, 23 Aug 1981, pp. 8–9. See also Roger Murray, 'What Leaked South Africa–US Papers Reveal', *New Africa* (London), Aug 1981, pp. 39–40.
2. Chester Crocker, 'South Africa: Strategy for Change', *Foreign Affairs*, vol. 50, no. 2 (Winter 1980–81) pp. 323–51.
3. 'Reagan and Africa', *Africa*, no. 111 (Nov 1980) p. 50.
4. *Economist* (London), 29 Mar 1981, p. 34.
5. *South Africa: Time Running Out*, report of the Rockefeller Foundation sponsored study commission on US policy toward Southern Africa (Berkeley, Calif.: University of California Press, 1981).
6. For details see El-Khawas and Cohen, *The Kissinger Study of Southern Africa*.
7. Merle Lipton, 'British Investment in South Africa: Is Constructive Engagement Possible?', *South Africa Labour Bulletin*, Oct 1976.
8. For details on SADCC see A. J. Nsekela (ed.), *Southern Africa: Towards Economic Liberation* (London: Rex Collings, 1981).

9. 'Aftermath of the Angolan Incursion', *West Africa*, 14 Sep 1981, pp. 2090–1. See also 'Angola Invaded', *West Africa*, 31 Aug 1981, p. 2020.
10. Harsch and Thomas, *Angola: The Hidden History of Washington's Secret War*, pp. 97–106.
11. 'An Assault on Angola', *Newsweek International* (New York), 7 Sep 1981, p. 13.
12. Murray, in *New Africa*, Aug 1981, p. 39.
13. Alexandre Mboukou, 'An African Triangle', *Africa Report* (New York), Sep-Oct 1982, p. 40.
14. Ibid.
15. 'Standing Firm on South Africa', *Christian Science Monitor* (Boston, Mass.), 16 Mar 1981, p. 28.
16. 'New American Line in South Africa', *West Africa*, 9 Mar 1981, p. 489.
17. Ibid.
18. *Economist*, 29 Mar 1981, p. 34.
19. *Peace Handbook: German African Possessions* (Wilmington, Del.: Scholarly Resources, 1973) p. 92.
20. Andrew R. Carlson, *German Foreign Policy, 1890–1914 and Colonial Policy to 1914: A Handbook and Annotated Bibliography* (Metuchen, NJ: Scarecrow Press, 1970) p. 53.
21. Allan D. Cooper, *US Economic Power and Political Influence in Namibia 1700–1982* (Boulder, Colo.: Westview, 1982) pp. 11–15.
22. Although this work has highlighted Nigeria's role in Southern African affairs, Nigeria's own domestic stability has been in doubt ever since it obtained independence in 1960. For the fifth time, Nigeria experienced a military coup in Dec 1983.
23. Elizabeth S. Landis and Michael Davis, 'Namibia: Impending Independence?' in *Southern Africa: The Continuing Crisis*, ed. G. M. Carter and P. O'Meara (Bloomington: Indiana University Press, 1979) p. 168.
24. *Yearbook of the United Nations* (New York: Department of Public Information, 1979) p. 282.
25. Cooper, *US Economic Power*, p. 54.
26. Marga Holness, 'Namibia: Pretoria hides behind Linkage', *Africa*, no. 133 (Sep 1982) pp. 35–6.
27. *Africa*, no. 111, p. 50.
28. On the mineral question, see 'Russia and Africa: The Mineral Connection', *Economist*, 9 July 1977, pp. 82–3. See also *South Africa: Time Running Out*, pp. 310–22.
29. *AF Press Clips* (Washington, DC), vol. XVI, no. 13 (27 Mar 1981) p. 17.
30. See *International Conference in Support of the Peoples of Zimbabwe and Namibia held in Maputo, Mozambique, 16–21 May 1977* (New York: UN Publications, May 1977) p. 10.
31. Steven Strasser and Holger Jensen, 'Zimbabwe: A Final, Priceless Reward', *Newsweek International* (New York), 28 April 1980, p. 12.
32. Ibid.
33. Gwendolyn M. Carter, 'Zimbabwe: The First Year', *Africa Report*, May–June 1981, p. 64.

34. Martin Rushmere, 'Zimbabwe Survey', *African Business* (London), May 1982, p. 63.
35. Ibid.
36. *South Africa: Time Running Out*, p. 325.
37. According to the US ambassador to the United Nations, Jeane Kirkpatrick, these acts led to a reduction of US aid to Zimbabwe.

NOTES TO CHAPTER SIX. CONCLUSION

1. Kwame Nkrumah, interview in *Time*, 20 July 1958.
2. At this juncture we should point out that the text here represents an integration of ideas and some credit should be given to Joel Samoff's essay 'Class, Class Conflicts and the State: Notes on the Political Economy of Africa', paper presented to the annual meeting of the African Studies Association in Houston, Texas, Nov 1977, published in *Political Science Quarterly*, Spring 1982.

Additional Bibliography

'Andrew Young and US Neo-Colonial Designs', *Southern Africa News* (Washington, DC) vol. 1, no. 2 (June 1977).

'The Andrew Young Affair'. *Newsweek*, 27 Aug 1979.

'The Black Backlash', *Newsweek*, Aug 1979.

Brzezinski, Zbigniew, *Between Two Ages* (New York: Viking, 1970).

Carpozi, George, *Andrew Young: The Impossible Man* (New York: Manor, 1978).

Clement, Lee, *Andrew Young at the United Nations* (Salisbury, NC: Documentary Publications, 1978).

'Collision Course over the PLO', *Newsweek*, 3 Sep 1979.

Cruse, Harold W., *The Crisis of the Negro Intellectual* (New York: William Morrow, 1967).

El-Khawas, Mohammed A., and Cohen, Barry, *The Kissinger Study of Southern Africa: National Security Study Memorandum 39* (Westport, Conn.: Lawrence Hill, 1976). The Kissinger study contains five policy options aimed at Southern Africa. These options follow an introduction which points out that the United States' $1500 million investment in Southern Africa is steadily rising.

Ellison, Julian, 'A Black US Lobby for Africa', *Africa*, May 1978.

'The Freezing of a Diplomat', *Africa*, Oct 1979.

Gardner, Carl, *Andrew Young* (New York: Drake, 1978).

Haskin, James, *Andrew Young: Man With a Mission* (New York: Lothrop, Lee and Shepard, 1979).

Hinds, Lennox, 'Political Prisoners in the United States', *Africa*, Sep 1978.

Johnson, Robert E., 'Ambassador Young's Last Official Trip to Africa', *Ebony*, Dec 1979.

Jordon, Phyllis P., 'The Apartheid System: Its Economic Dimension', paper presented at the Afro–American Museum Seminar on South Africa, Southgate, Michigan, 4 June 1977.

Madhubuti, Haki R., *Enemies: The Clash of Races* (Chicago: Third World Press, 1978), esp. the chapter entitled 'Sixth Pan-African Congress: What is Being Done to Save the Black Race?'

Marable, Manning, 'Tuskegee, Alabama: The Politics of Illusion in the New South', *Black Scholar*, vol. 8, no. 7 (May 1977) pp. 13–24.

Mboukou, Alexandre, 'An African Triangle', *Africa Report*, Sep–Oct 1982.

Nkrumah, Kwame, *Neo-Colonialism: The Last Stage of Imperialism* (New York: International Publishers, 1966).

Onyeani, Chika, 'US Black Enterprise and Business in Africa', *Africa*, Aug 1978.

Pratt, Cranford, *The Critical Phases in Tanzania 1945–1968* (Cambridge: Cambridge University Press, 1976).

Stone, Eddie, *Andrew Young: Biography of a Realist* (Los Angeles: Holloway House, 1980).

Usman, Yusufu Bala, *For the Liberation of Nigeria* (London: New Beacon, 1979).

Western Massachusetts Association of Concerned African Scholars, *US Military Involvement in Southern Africa* (Dar es Salaam: Tanzania Publishing House; and Boston, Mass.: South End Press, 1978).

Young, Andrew, 'Economic Development', *Ivy Leaf*, Fall 1982, pp. 9–11.

Index